Closer By The Mile

The story of the Pan-Mass Challenge, vanguard in the fight against cancer

KEN BRACK

Float Tide Publications
Plympton, Ma

The Hucks' Bike Route

BALLSTON SPA
HUCKLEBERRY START

Augmenting the Pan-Massachusetts Challenge bike-a-thon for cancer, riders on Team Huckleberry started from upstate New York in 2011. They rode an extra 184 miles for eight-year-old Hannah Hughes of Ballston Spa, who was in treatment for a rare type of leukemia. Two days later, the Hucks joined five thousand riders at the main start in Sturbridge, Ma., to begin the official PMC weekend. They continued to the Cape Cod Canal, and then on to the Provincetown finish on day four. The Hucks rode 371 miles and started again from Hannah's driveway in 2012.

WEST
STOCKBRIDGE

STURBRIDGE
PMC START

○ TEAM HUCKLEBERRY ROUTE

● MAIN PMC ROUTES

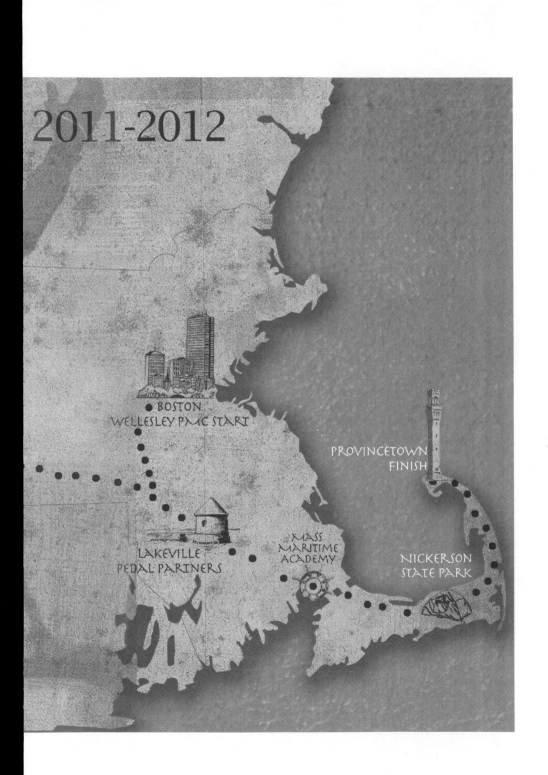

Prologue

At the 158th mile I blew off a shortcut to the finish line. Straight ahead would bring us in. A right took us to the Province Lands with its dry scrub pine and steep dunes curling around Race Point. This was the climactic rise I'd heard about, the place where riders summon their ultimate strength.

Asshole. From perhaps ten yards behind, Denise swore at me as I made the turn, pretending not to see the sign. Other riders were stopped by the turnoff waiting for friends. Consulting with each other, at least. We still had another five miles up some of the toughest hills.

She had pedaled a road bike for two days, the first one through nearly 100 percent humidity, and this morning into a short downpour. We started in Wellesley, a Boston suburb. And here was Provincetown, bathed in brilliant August light. Stellwagen Bank lay to the north with its leviathans feeding in a placid bay. We had biked together all summer and much of the spring, discovering lush backroads, noticing the doorways of old farmhouses, their blinking bullseye windows, and preparing for the weekend. We rode for my mom, Joan. Surely smiling at us.

Yet I ignored her whisper. Wait for Denise. Trust her.

I heard my wife call out after we rounded the corner. Slowing to the side, I unclipped my shoes and planted my feet.

"What are you doing?" she piqued.

"This is the way."

"Did you not see the shortcut? I know you did." Fire and ice.

"We have to go this way," I said. "*This* is what it's all about." Knowing, as the words skidded out, that I was absolutely wrong.

She clipped in again and started off.

"You could've asked."

I followed, then moved to her side. For much of the weekend, for most of our 25 years actually, we'd been pretty much in synch. I was a jerk again. She was spent. The hills of North Wellfleet and Truro, in the sun's glare, had taken their toll. Done with a so-called partner trying to tell her what to think, where to go.

I must have groaned myself considering the next grade up ahead. As we climbed again, five young guys overtook us.

They wore identical riding jerseys and sleek pants all the color of rosa rugosa, the beach rose I associate with places my mother loved best. Each outfit was imprinted with ribbons of varied colors denoting different types of cancer — jade, lavender, hot pink, cranberry, lime green. As each rider passed, his encouragement rolled off:

"You got this, almost there...You got this...Nice job!"

The thing was, they really meant it. I looked back, not too far now, and she was locked in again, her olive-skinned face taught and scrunched down under a red and gray helmet. Her eyes, shielded by sunglasses, may have still been throwing daggers. Around us the dunes rose up to ridges draped like scarfs over a lunar landscape; I had a fleeting feeling of motionlessness in an unmapped terrain. We plodded up, barely keeping momentum forward. I realized this was the last hill. Then, like sailors who encounter the first fecund swell of land as they approach it from downwind, a wash of cool air off the ocean embraced us.

Denise and I regrouped as always. And finally, what mattered most was so much more than the ride itself.

Chapter One

Lovefest

The occasion, a bike-a-thon to end cancer, was created by a guy named Billy Starr. It quickly grew into a mid-summer lovefest, which is fine with him. As long as people keep giving even more than they get.

One Friday night during August in 2009, Starr mounted an auditorium podium in central Massachusetts. He wore a powder blue polo shirt and khaki shorts. Lean and of medium height, with thick strawberry-blonde hair in a layered cut that's parted in the middle, Starr knew exactly how to command attention. He always has.

Several thousand cyclists and volunteers faced him and the multi-colored banners fanning each side of the stage. On the cusp of this weekend, the Sturbridge Host Hotel had transformed into a campus beehive. Wedged beside a pond amidst the hills of Worcester County, its parking lots were overtaken by bike racks, trailers, and people checking their gear. Cow bells rang in a brief delirious clamor as each first-timer registered. Riders in shorts and sandals, mostly white professionals of all ages, greeted each other in chow lines and under a massive tent. Inside, on this evening of anticipatory celebration, the crowd hushed.

He looked out and briefly flashed his eyes down to his notes. "I want you to know that tonight is an extremely emotional and humbling night for me," he began. "Your commitment is unrivaled."

Starr named it the Pan-Massachusetts Challenge for the inaugural ride back in 1980. Now the Pan-Mass, or PMC as it is best known, was kicking off its 30th year. Come sunrise, riders would mount their seats for a two-day trek as far as 192 miles. Winding through old mill towns and shaded backroads to cranberry bogs and estuaries on the coastal plain, most participants eagerly submit to a gritty physical challenge. As swarms of cyclists move along, they are reinvigorated by pulsing throngs on the roadsides, who together spark a circuitry of psychic goodwill. Teens banging drums and pans, neighbors on a corner doing their wave. Kids with cardboard signs supporting a neighbor's ride, or a young boy in treatment for a rare leukemia. A woman in a beige sunhat on her lawn as the rain begins, who simply says, "Be safe today."

It is not a race. More of a marathon. Which is most fitting, given the epic nature of all this. The PMC, as the bike-a-thon is known best, takes place on a single weekend in a relatively small state. Yet its impact is singular and often astonishingly direct, if not exponential, in the forging of new cures. The event Starr founded at his dad's dining room table contributes millions of dollars each year to cancer care and research at the Dana-Farber Cancer Institute in Boston. It raised $375 million in the first 33 years, becoming the most successful single-event athletic fundraiser in the country. As Starr occasionally extolls, there is no receding tide in sight, as the event broke its own record in 2012. It is Dana-Farber's largest funding source. The PMC provides just over half of the annual revenue for the Jimmy Fund, the institute's fundraising arm and namesake of the renowned pediatric clinic at DFCI-Boston Children's Hospital.

Among the legions of cancer centers doing clinical research and providing patient care, DFCI and the other preeminent teaching hospitals it partners with are often in the vanguard of achieving breakthroughs. Together they speed the development of new drugs and a deeper understanding of genetic abnormalities, which help scientists increasingly match therapies to each cancer's genetic makeup. Their practitioners give families hope where there was once mainly churning fear. Their patients and the many survivors, lifted by loved ones, give back in extraordinary ways.

At times, with the PMC's backing, Dana-Farber is able to take risks on promising yet so-called fringe research it otherwise could not afford. The results, while wrenching for those touched by a wide range of diseases—from pediatric solid tumors to intestinal, breast and ovarian cancers—are often heartening. Practitioners call it the magic money. The PMC allows them to conduct research and clinical trials and add advanced treatment rooms. "To take people who are creative and bright-eyed and desirous to work and do something special," says Dr. Lee Nadler, Dean for Clinical and Translational Research at Harvard Medical School. He is also a long-time PMC rider. "That was me 30 years ago."

Most of what the event raises comes in as unrestricted gifts. This allows DFCI flexibility to meet needs as it sees fit. Yet some riders also find solace and inspiration by earmarking their donations to specific research groups in honor of loved ones. A Connecticut couple whose son battles neuroblastoma started a riding team that is among the frontrunners in aiding doctors and researchers of that disease. A survivor of osteosarcoma, which claimed his right leg as a teenager, continues to defy negative prognosticators by swimming and riding to fund a researcher. Friends of a young Bostonian who lost her life to Ewing's Sarcoma support related discoveries by bone and sarcoma oncologists.

Regardless of the way more than 5,000 cyclists choose to give, their sweat is refreshed and reinforced each year by more than 3,000 volunteers. Retirees who slice cantaloupe at water stops, guys repairing flat tires, and the kid who approaches you at a rest stop with a water jug in one hand and Gatorade in the other. Together they bring the promise of life to tens of thousands. While it can be so damning to experience relatives and friends suffering from disease, perhaps even this is surmountable. As a woman in her 50s told my wife and I before starting out, "Riding gives me a chance to do something." The event is a crescendo of giving, not in volume alone, but those reaching out to support each other's gifts at such an elemental level. It fuels many of us to go a little further.

To do this, much is asked of participants and everyone behind the scenes. They continue to deliver at astonishing levels. Riders from 36 states each make a $4,300 minimum contribution for the most popular routes, an amount guaranteed by credit card. Many far exceed this donation.

The average amount raised per rider grew from $1,370 in 1990 to $6,500 in 2011, and it jumped again a year later to $6,900. Sprain an ankle on the first day and you still owe the minimum; neither couples riding together nor Living Proof survivors receive a break. With corporate sponsors and in-kind donors amplifying this commitment and covering expenses, every rider dollar raised goes right to Dana-Farber.

The wizard of this rising energy, a progenitor in Teva sandals, is a guy who for most of his life has thrived on pushing himself to physical extremes outdoors. Until recently he would gleefully measure up crags for rock-hopping even while on vacation with his wife and their two young daughters.

Yet as Billy Starr looked out from the Sturbridge podium that night, he truly centered himself. Starr knew that in a sense the event actually did not originate with him. The PMC's reach transcended what he could have imagined in his late 20s, when the notion finally came.

While the event "evolved from significant personal experiences in my life," Starr continued, "I'm actually acutely aware that everyone of you has a personal story, an important story, that brought you here...I simply provided a vehicle for this generosity of spirit to be expressed.

"What I am today and who I've become can be traced back to the demise and death of my mother. Some people know exactly why they are who they are, and how they got there. I'm one of them ... at least now I am."

He was always a willful kid with a rascal's glint in his eye.

Before entering kindergarten, Billy was leader of his neighborhood pack around Hagen Road in Newton Centre, thick in Boston's suburbs. He convinced his pals once to dam a nearby brook with sticks. They went at it until Billy's mom Betty came down and scolded them in her stern way, "What are you doing?!" Another time his older brother Mark chased Billy around the streets when he was supposed to be on a bus for nursery school. "He climbed a tree and just wouldn't come down," Mark Starr remembers. "When Billy got an idea it was really hard to dissuade him." It was the mid-50s, a time when kids ran free down the street and through parks, and in and out of neighbors' houses.

Billy was bossy and brash. He wanted people to listen to him, and it didn't sit well when they didn't. Stuart Silverman grew up down the street and went toe-to-toe with his friend a few times. In seventh-grade they were playing football in Silverman's yard against some older guys, including Mark. "We got into an argument and I was standing up to him," Silverman says. "His brother appreciated that someone finally said, 'You can't be the boss all the time.'"

Playing for his junior high football team, Billy took it upon himself to change a play. With the score tied at 0-0 and about a minute left in the game, it was fourth down near their own end line. The coach sent Billy in to punt. He was a second-string quarterback, convinced that his arm was good enough to be a starter. A teammate suggested they try a fake. So Billy said, "That's what we're going to do." His pass attempt failed, the other team scored and won. The next Monday at practice, as the coach lectured the squad he spotted the upstart smiling at him—Silverman describes it as a smirk, but Billy remains adamant it was not. The coach kicked him off the team. "Maybe he was looking for a reason," Silverman cracks.

"It was naive and arrogant to counter the coach's orders," Starr remembers. "I recognize it now. I knew I was going to be in trouble." He adds, "It was a weekend-long delayed execution."

From an early age Starr was also very loyal to friends. Even if the result meant injury, he was unafraid to take risks for what he considered the right thing. In sixth grade some guys a few years older stole his baseball cards. Billy led Silverman and some others, including Mark, over to a house to get them back. "We got pummeled," Stuart says, "but he wasn't afraid." When a friend got cut from the junior high basketball team Billy organized a petition drive. The entire team signed it, and he presented it to the coach. Teammate Billy Levine was brought back. "I guess this is the reason he's been successful," Silverman says. "He was his own man—sort of." If his brother didn't get what he wanted, Mark agrees, "there was hell to pay."

Being headstrong is a trait Starr received from his mother. Lithe and lean, Betty Finkel Starr was a head turner but no pushover. If a group of girls walked into a room, she was the one you looked at first, longtime friends recall. With wavy blonde hair and a tightly drawn face, she was striking enough to work for a time as an agency model. While usually warm and tender towards her sons and their friends, Betty had a steely backbone cast during the Depression. When she said no, discussion was over. She was also very proper. Even as jeans came in style in the 50s, she admonished her sister-in-law to dress right when she went shopping.

Billy's dad Milton was more of a teddy bear. Honest and a little paunchy, he enjoyed eating out and could spin a hilarious story. He was one of those people whom everyone loves. As their house became a magnet for the neighborhood kids Milton never seemed to mind. He made them feel at home whether watching in torment as Bucky Dent's unlikely home run sank the Red Sox, or when Mark's college friends piled in after a hockey tournament to sleep on the rugs. Despite Billy's occasional mischief, his father had a hard time maintaining any anger towards him. "If he spanked us," Mark says, "it was, 'This hurts me more than it hurts you.' It really was with him." He could also be a father of stealth, who would show up unannounced at his son's game. He was restrained and perceptive. In a fashion very different than his wife's, Milton would play an indirect role in the PMC's story, providing unconditional support in its fledgling years.

Betty and Milton Starr matured in that era when enduring extreme hardships and sacrifice wasn't heralded. It was just raw daily reality. Her parents were both first-generation American Jews whose families had emigrated from Russia, and likely the Ukraine beginning in the late 1800s. They were prosperous, at least for a while. Betty's maternal grandparents, Joseph and Dora Frank, raised a family in Burlington, Vermont, amidst a small Russian Jewish community. One son moved up from being a peddler and junk dealer to owning several clothing stores, and their father helped found a synagogue in 1887. The ninth of ten children, Betty's mother Rachel went to college like each of her siblings, majoring in German at the University of Vermont, where she was captain of the tennis team. She became the first Jewish student inducted into UVM's "mortar board," a college honorary society. But for her, those successes were short-lived.

Rachel married Joseph Finkel, who had attended Boston Latin Academy and Harvard and soon appeared to be comfortably ensconced as a stockbroker. Their only daughter was born into wealth in 1924 and the family lived in a plush Upper West Side apartment near the Museum of Natural History. But Finkel lost everything in the market crash. They were forced to move in to a maid's chambers at her aunt's home. Consumed by shame, Joseph never fully recovered. Despite his education and upbringing, he still ultimately failed. Eventually they quit New York for Brookline, Massachusetts, living in a dank and unfurnished apartment in the relatively hard-scrabble Riverside area near the rail lines. While two of his brothers remained very successful—one was an obstetrician—Finkel could not afford to send his only daughter to college. She was the first woman in the family unable to attend university, as her aunts were also college educated. "A staggering reversal," Mark Starr says.

Longtime girlfriends Janet Ginns and Barbara Fine met Betty at a hall in Cleveland Circle where weekend dances were held. She was a standout, easily becoming the most popular in their group, even though Betty went to Brookline High, while Janet and Barbara both attended private schools. Betty's friends didn't dwell upon the Finkel's relative distress. Betty went to work early supporting her parents, continuing this throughout her married life. "She never complained, ever," Fine says. "She lived such a different life from the rest of us. Whatever she made, she gave to her parents." She waited in bread lines as her father sought work, and eventually he landed a low-level clerk's job. Her mother suffered from depression. "Her parents were not really capable," Mark adds. "The real question was why didn't he bounce back?" Betty's uncle, Dr. Finkel, also provided support for the family. Far from being insensitive to the demands on their daughter, Rachel and Joseph doted on her as best they could. When she came home from school or work, Betty's mother insisted that she lie down and rest.

Betty worked as a secretary for the Red Cross and helped Ginns get her first job out of college. Janet, who had studied sociology at Smith College, was hired to write personal histories of soldiers who had suffered mental breakdowns and been institutionalized. Her other friends also had college degrees, and Betty modeled for a while at the prestigious Powers Agency in

New York. Yet her destiny was back close to Boston where Ginns and their friends were dating some of the Starr boys.

The oldest of four brothers, Milton and his family made it through their own successive trials, as each son joined the Army, went overseas during World War II and returned. Their father Max Starr had emigrated from the Kiev area of Ukraine, but not with his parents, who were apparently property owners. When they arrived later in America, any sentimentalities for the old country were plowed under, as they rarely spoke of their past life. Max started a business in 1913 doing fine millwork, and it is believed he met his wife Sarah, also from Russia, around the same time. He built showcases, bars and other cabinetry, raising his family in Boston's Mattapan and Roxbury neighborhoods. Later under the helm of his sons and a third generation, Boston Showcase Company grew into a large restaurant equipment supplier.

Born in 1915, Milton graduated from tiny Franklin & Marshall College, a modest liberal arts school in Pennsylvania. While he may have been interested in medicine, he didn't have the grades, nor did the college have anything near the pedigree of the Ivy schools his brothers would attend. He had a very good time there, and accounts of his exploits given to Betty's girlfriends left them in stitches. Famously, and with true good humor, he'd later crack that among his siblings, "One brother went to Harvard, another to Yale, another went to UPenn, and I..." He undoubtedly also believed that as the oldest son, his duty was to his father's business. Soon after graduating college in 1938 Milton was working for his father as a salesman, and by 1940 Max and Sarah had moved the family out to Chestnut Hill.

Milton entered the Army in the first draft before Pearl Harbor and did infantry training. While stationed at Fort Devens, he was a mess officer who trained infantry. Apparently he looked ahead and didn't like his odds. Starr asked an old friend named Jay Ginns for help. Ginns, Janet's future husband, had been Milton's counselor at a summer camp in Maine called Indian Acres. Ginns was four or five years older and took Milton under his wing at camp. This gesture ushered in a combination of camaraderie and outdoor experiences that would infuse the Starr family legacy for at least two generations.

By 1942 Ginns was a dentist and a captain in the Army's Medical Administrative Corps, which was in dire need of medical officers. The Army was pushing them through training at the Carlisle Barracks in Pennsylvania. Jay was high up and oversaw the teaching there. Milton asked, "What can you do for me?" Ginns knew the Surgeon General, the top authority, who plucked Starr out of the infantry. He transferred to Medical Field Service School, which ran its charges through a tough three-month course, and then served as a lieutenant in the medical corps in Europe.

Brothers Erwin, Leonard and Jason followed suit. Erwin, the next oldest, was a major who likely saw combat in the Battle of the Bulge. Leonard went into intelligence serving under General MacArthur and was recalled during the Korean War to break code. Youngest brother Jason joined late as a private in the Infantry Engineering Corps helping to build bridges. He was at sea en route to Japan when the war ended. "To him it was the greatest thing that ever happened," his wife says. "It was the greatest experience in his life and something he always talked about with joy." Each one made it home.

Milton experienced the front lines, supervising stretcher bearers among other duties. Like most who had seen enough of war, Starr didn't talk much about it with his sons. Mark recalls once asking his dad about a citation that he kept in the basement. It was from the French government. Milton simply said, "It was for getting his men lost in enemy territory, and then getting them back safely."

He was on hand for one of the war's most emotional triumphs, the liberation of Paris on August 25, 1944. It was a moment of divine exaltation for French and American troops mobbed by Parisians who had staged the risky final uprising. Starr was assigned as a liaison with French Maj. General Philippe Leclerc's Second Armored Division, having embedded with it for about four months. The division missed D-Day, crossing the Channel almost two months later to assist the Allied advance in a maneuver surrounding the Germans in Normandy. Its key mission was to lead the charge into the City of Light. A few weeks later, despite missteps and Leclerc's defiance of his American superiors, the general sent in a small detachment that took over a hotel in the middle of the city just before midnight. Word spread quickly, as the historian Martin Blumenson recorded:

> *The bells of nearby Notre Dame began to ring joyously. Another church took up the refrain and then another. Soon all the churches in Paris were ringing their bells in celebration. A cascade of sound washed over the city.*

Not many Parisians had gone to sleep that night. The telephones had been working, and everyone knew that soldiers were in the suburbs. The bells of the churches could mean only one thing: The liberators had arrived.

Starr didn't linger long to celebrate. While Ernest Hemingway reportedly popped champagne at another hotel, Milton had to leave for reassignment the next day.

Years later he would tell his sons, perhaps half-jokingly, that he never ate better than when he dined as an officer with the French. But he didn't say much about Paris. Nor about Leclerc, or the general's skepticism of Patton and other American commanders. Nor of the fighting in a pocket of Normandy. Milton's father was sick, and as the oldest son he was discharged a little early in 1945 before Max Starr's death. His life's work would be the business and later, raising two sons. Sometime during the war he met Betty.

The Starr boys were marrying off. Like so many returning GIs, they were in a rush to find partners. The fates of several of Betty Finkel's girlfriends and the Starrs became intertwined. Some of the gals had known the brothers since their teen years; Janet and Leonard were in the same confirmation class at their temple and dated briefly. Erwin and Leonard went first, marrying on the same weekend home on leave with their oldest brother standing in as best man for both. Leonard married Betty's good friend Alma from Newton. After the ceremony Milton introduced his pal Jay Ginns to

Milton and Betty Starr.

Janet. Ginns proposed to her the same night. "There was always a shortage of men," Janet notes. "He was tall, dark, and handsome. And then I found out he was very bright."

At some point Milton and Betty became a serious couple. Mark believes they may have met at a party. They married in June of 1946, holding their reception at the Hotel Kenmore close to Fenway Park. Starting out was not easy, as Milton's mother Sarah moved in. Betty also needed to learn how to cook. There were many burned dishes and accidents, which exasperated her new husband. He may have been a bit harsh in

Billy Starr with his mother Betty.

those early moments, but Milton absolutely adored her. First son Mark arrived in 1947, and Billy in the spring of 1951.

With Milton as president, each of the four Starr men entered their father's business: Erwin and Jason went into sales, while Leonard handled orders from inside. They expanded into food service equipment and began kitchen design for big accounts like Harvard and some hotel chains. The brothers ate lunch daily at the Hotel Somerset on Commonwealth Avenue, not far from their office. The four couples stayed close, often eating out on Friday nights at the Somerset, and later at Anthony's Pier 4, another business client. "We are a very unusual family," says Billy's aunt Betty, who married Jason. "We all got along." Gatherings with great food and wine became a tradition that was passed down whether to celebrate the Jewish holidays or mark the end of another work week.

While comfortable, life for Billy's family was generally modest. There were excursions to Nantasket Beach, where friends had a house, summer camp for the boys and private boarding school for Mark. His parents sent Mark there because they felt he was underachieving in public school. Billy flat out refused to go to that route; besides, Newton South High was just up the street. "It was the end of discussion because when Billy said, 'No way,' it wasn't going to happen," his brother says.

Their home typified the middle-class enclave of garrisons and colonials with its three bedrooms, white siding and black shutters. Few neighbors built fences and the kids dashed through backyards as if they were on the sidewalk. They enjoyed a few perks but nothing lavish. Milton added an above-ground pool when his wife began having back troubles. He and his brothers bought Patriots season tickets, at first bringing their wives and then successive sons and cousins back when the young Pats played at Fenway, or at BU and Harvard Stadium. The families continued as season ticket holders for 52 years. Infrequently, Milton and Betty took a vacation to Europe or the Caribbean, but not extended family trips, and many years they skipped a vacation. Still, Billy felt fortunate enough going to the Indian Acres camp for 13 years—they kept him out one summer in high school because of bad grades. As her kids grew, Betty remained frugal. She continued to bank money for her parents, working at Brandeis as a secretary. She kept shopping at Loehmann's rather than bigger-name department stores even as Milton did well.

Milton Starr with sons Mark, left, and Billy.

Most of all, their mother's overarching decency affected her sons deeply. In the late 50s and early 60s she volunteered helping children with cerebral palsy. She also visited disabled veterans. Many were paraplegics and quadriplegics, spitting out their bitterness and bile against those trying to help. Mark went once with her to the veterans hospital. He didn't return. The men's nastiness drove many volunteers away after a few weeks—but not all of them, and not his mom.

"She broke through it," Mark says. "Our house was filled with paintings and ashtrays and things the vets made for her, mostly using their teeth."

"In the course of one's life," Billy continued in that PMC opening ceremonies speech, "chaos or the unexpected may change one's course or destination, maybe for an hour, maybe forever. We have to look in the mirror and recognize who is looking back at us."

Billy first looked hard into that mirror when his mother died of melanoma cancer. Betty was only 49, and he was 23. Losing her set Starr on a new path that was guided by his drive for exhilarating physical challenges and his parents' unconditional faith in him. Ultimately he turned his grief into action, and the cycling event he cooked up helped transform how we give back.

It was 1973 and the first squall of his life was about to rip. Billy graduated from the University of Denver with a bachelor's degree in political science and an English minor. But he'd really excelled in rock climbing and skiing. His itinerary included a trip to climb the Himalayas. Back home three months post graduation, after playing in a tennis tournament one day he walked into his father crying in the bedroom. Billy had never seen him do this before. "Mom is going to die," his dad told him. When Betty had some moles removed a few years earlier, there was little need to tell Billy and Mark. They hadn't known about a bunch of benign tumors either, which were now malignant. Milton also had tried to protect his wife from the truth until it was too late.

Mark Starr, whose distinguished career as a journalist would include three decades covering foreign and national affairs and sports at *Newsweek*, was just about to start a job with *The Wall Street Journal* in Chicago. He returned when he could, while Billy shelved his trekking plans to stay home. When Betty was treated at Massachusetts General Hospital in and out that fall and winter, he and his dad visited her three times a day, five days a week. He took a job driving a truck at Boston Showcase. They ate together and mixed Jack Daniel's Manhattans into their routine—two at dinner, five times a week. "After the second Manhattan we found something to smile about," Billy recalls. "It was a tough year."

In that era many American families just didn't talk about a terminal illness and their grief, even relatively open ones like the Starrs. And physicians didn't automatically inform patients of a prognosis. One time at the hospital, Mark recalls his mother asking a young doctor—perhaps a resident covering on the weekend, not her primary one—"'Why don't I feel any better?' And he said, 'You may never feel any better.' I think that's the first time she had any idea." Similarly, Betty and Milton never sat their sons down to have the big talk about their future after she passed, or the parents' aspirations. She knew they were well grounded, and giving speeches was not her style. "There was no Hollywood moment," BIlly says. Just as she and her husband hadn't talked much about their family histories, they didn't openly discuss the present crisis.

Her health declined rapidly, and the family's worries were compounded by the sudden loss of Milton's brother Leonard, who was very close to Billy especially, and also a first cousin. Cancer claimed both men. Leonard, the former intelligence officer, was compassionate and brilliant. He died of a brain tumor about a year before Betty did, and losing his uncle shook Billy up. Leonard didn't have any sons, and he had spent a fair amount of time with Billy, taking him to an art museum for the first time as a kid. Leonard was the first of that generation to go, and the start of what Starr calls "the dying that takes down everybody." Then his mom's death on the first day of June in 1974 devastated the three Starr men. Billy's world shrunk, his wanderlust squelched. "I was having nightmares and just couldn't be who I had remembered myself to be prior to my mother's death. I got to see the darker side of life, this cocky inexperienced kid. This was making me more humble, and I didn't like it." It crushed his sweet and doting father, who never really recovered. Around the same time Milton developed Parkinson's disease. Although illness wasn't the driving factor, he was forced to retire a few years later.

Starr tried on undersized jobs and made countless backpacking treks before discovering his direction. He lived mostly at home and largely floundered. He tried life as a reporter, worked in public relations and got a master's degree in social work. Babson College hired him as the squash coach. Yet Billy was too assertive to work for anyone else, and those things didn't fulfill him.

What did were physical challenges, occasionally extreme ones. At some point he began going on really long bike rides, sometimes 140 miles from

Newton to Provincetown, often alone. "I was just doing it for the beer," he recalls. "I would get up early in the morning and go catch the 3:30 ferry home. I didn't have a credit card." He'd hitchhike back if needed. He'd also bike alone from Williamstown to the Lower Cape, the longest way traversing the state, some 300 miles. He enlisted friends for the P-town rides.

Finding meaning was a struggle. At 23 or 24, he wrote an autobiography called "Great Potential," never published. The mere mention of it drives his old friend Silverman into cackling. "And this was before he did a thing!" Silverman spurts, then recalls more seriously, "I had the sense he was lost." Many years later, Billy reflected on this time with that audience in Sturbridge. His own grief "was like a raft that sent me into uncharted waters that were my transformation," he told them. "Six years on I tried unsuccessfully to balance my sense of profound loss with my sense of adulthood."

When his epiphany finally came, Starr's growth curve—his true passion and art—was about to take off. In the spring of 1980 Billy was riding through the blooming nurseries of the Arnold Arboretum in Jamaica Plain at dusk and, "Literally a light went on. I remember very well thinking, 'I'm going to do a bike ride.'" Not many people were doing athletic fundraising then, but he saw something out there. His first thought was persuading people to donate for every mile he rode himself.

Crossing the state on a bicycle to fight cancer. An outlandish notion. First he'd have to be a persistent nag. He approached the Jimmy Fund, which for New Englanders has been synonymous with the Red Sox ever since its first big sponsor, the National League Boston Braves, left for Milwaukee in 1953. PMC lore has it that Mike Andrews, the former Sox infielder who was just beginning his long tenure as Jimmy Fund chairman, laughed when Starr first approached him with the idea. Someone else asked Starr, "What's really your goal?" He said, "To raise money for cancer research." "You think you can do this better by yourself?" They wished him good luck. He realized it couldn't be a solo effort.

Billy became an irritant to the Jimmy Fund brass, a mosquito who'd always find his way around the hand slaps, and over the years this endeared him to them. Chris McKeown, a longtime rider and Starr's early

*Pals Ken Shulman and Dave Hellman
with Starr on the Appalachian Trail
in May, 1976.*

right hand man, remembers standoffish meetings with Andrews checking his watch. Amy Bresky, an original volunteer and Starr's friend, adds, "It was, thanks if you hand us a check, but don't look to us for advertising or promoting." Andrews says it was clear that Starr had all the right intentions. "I never imagined in my wildest dreams, I didn't see it as big as some of the other things we had on the table," he says. "It dwarfed them all."

When he returned from pressing the flesh with his idea, Billy sat down at Milton's table and began painting on a very large landscape. Loving the challenge of strenuous rides, he would demand a similar grit from each participant. He worked 15 years from the house before moving into an office. What started as Starr's tribute to his mother's memory became her gift to him.

It's no surprise to anyone who meets Starr that the great allegories of his life occurred outdoors, sometimes as he pushed himself and his friends to their limits. Long rides such as up Mount Washington were one thing. Another seminal event was a 400-mile hiking trip on the Appalachian Trail a few years after his mother died. The trip taught him what happens when there is no buy-in from others. Billy planned the entire trek for three friends, mailing supplies to post offices along the route. It was still mud season when they started at the end of the AT on Mount Katahdin, even though Baxter State Park was officially still closed. After one sunny day it rained for eight straight. Everyone's endurance was put to the test.

Old friend Dave Hellman will never forget. They slogged through a lot of water, one hiker's feet got trashed; it wasn't extreme cold, but nasty still. Two guys quit. "Billy had no sign of letting up. He said, 'Let's go.'" Hellman remembers. "I said, 'Okay, I'll keep going,' but from my perspective if he'd hung it up, I wouldn't have minded."

They made a hairy river crossing, walked hours on a trail completely immersed in water, and slept in lean-to's. But they kept on moving. In one mystical moment, still deep in the Maine woods, a woman came out of a hut offering steaming cups of coffee. "To me she was an angel, 'cause I needed it. I needed help," Starr told a reporter years later. Near the end, their friends rejoined them and as they crossed into New Hampshire stayed one night in a comfortable A-frame. "In hindsight there is something special in all that rain. He just did it," Hellman says.

What Starr gleaned from the trip he later applied to the PMC. Lesson one: he had done everything; the others weren't vested in it. "Make them share the work," he says. This led to an inventive practice of requiring riders to give their credit card information in advance of registering; by 2012, the minimum commitment was $4,300 per rider. The adoption of the credit card policy cut down delinquency to one percent; disgruntled wanna-riders need not apply. Lesson two: the woman in the woods who brought coffee. "She answered the need," he says. "So I never forgot that. I knew that by creating this bike event, I'd create some pain, and I had to fill the need." Commitment became his platform, and a community of riders began to grow.

He has relayed these key experiences in public many times. When I first met Starr one morning at his office—a modest, communal space in the throat of an industrial park where most of the staff shares one room connected to a warehouse—he seemed not to mind reminiscing again. He dipped back: "I was resourceful. I was also mischievous and sort of liked creating challenges, which if it didn't work out, then it got interesting." As he formed that last phrase his eyes glinted and he cracked a Dennis-the-Menace smile which seemed to be both natural and somewhat practiced, yet still not calibrated. I looked at his spare room, a throwback. It reminded me of an unkempt college newspaper editor's den: folders stacked against the wall; few accessories, no bookcases or file cabinets; the focus clearly his computer monitor and keyboard on a desk otherwise largely cleared. A few treasured photos lurked around including one of him throwing out a ball at Fenway Park. He dressed in jeans and a gray casual shirt, occasionally propping white running shoes on his desk. Clearly not a button-down guy, but no one would confuse him with being terribly laid back, either.

In 1980 Starr pushed on with his notion, handing out leaflets on bike paths and cajoling his biking buddies. He conjured the route from AAA maps and old ones he found in a library. That September the first 36 riders took off from a Springfield shopping mall in thick fog, the first leg of what began as a strange, looping trip.

Billy was dating Amy Bresky's younger sister, and he asked Amy to help at that first ride. She was one of four volunteers. Amy ran a construction company and was a one-woman PMC road crew, showing up in a Ford dump body pickup loaded with tools, chicken salad sandwiches, water jugs, lawn chairs, her bicycle, and her 18-year-old tenant. In those days, there were no water stops—that was Bresky in the truck trying to leapfrog cyclists. With poor signage and the weather, many of the red shirts quickly got lost. Two women ended up in Medford, way off course north of the city.

Barry Kraft, a boyhood friend of Starr's who has ridden every year and whose son Zak would later survive cancer, recalls riding beside a woman at a modest pace. They didn't finish the first day in Plymouth until 7:30 p.m. When they met up with a poor soul whose job was driving a mini van that had "PMC" written on it with provisions for riders, there was little food left for lunch. By supper, it was hamburger buns sans burgers. "I swore to Billy I would never do it again," Kraft says, "but as it turns out, it was the best thing I ever did." There was also no communication. Cell phones were just a distant tease, CBs and ham radios weren't used to relay messages until the next year. They went 140 miles the first day, Billy got diarrhea after a lunch of fried clams, while Amy drove the truck back and down and back looking for riders. They raised $10,200 after a total 220 miles.

"This was truly a seat of the pants creation—make it up as you go," Bresky says. "Billy's always been the big picture guy. He went around asking friends, will you help me with this idea? At first it was basic, no route, no nothing. I have no idea how many riders got the chicken salad."

Billy is often asked about his reaction to that first weekend. He doesn't exactly remember, except that on a bus back to Boston (the ferry broke down), he overheard someone say, "Next year, we'll improve." It struck him then that he lacked a business plan. Yet, "I heard what it meant to other people, this thing that a bike event could absolutely be an extension of a person." That night he told his former girlfriend, "'I think I can make this big.' 'That's nice,' she said, 'but grow up.' That's when I decided, I've got to make this work." A few others like Bresky weren't sure there would be a second. But for those not completely slumped over with exhaustion, the first of many parties broke out.

To some of Starr's relatives and his dad's friends, the first time was a lark. One of his aunts, Betty Starr, who shares his mom's given name and was close with her, recalls that after floundering around, Billy "just came upon this. All of us were like, 'Ah-h-h, this will just last a year, and then he'll move on to something else.' Whatever he did, he did right and it just happened. And he built it up with incredible skill."

After the maiden ride, friends who wrote Starr confirmed his belief that not only were the riders helping others, "but the PMC simply helped

Legendary PMCer Todd Miller, left, with longtime riders and pals Barry Kraft, center, and Ted Merritt.

the people giving to feel good." The next year, he switched the start to Sturbridge cutting the distance by 25 miles, and more than 200 riders raised $40,600. Later they moved the date back to August. What felt like a camp reunion in the peak of summer began taking hold.

When Starr handed the Jimmy Fund his second check—a 400 percent jump—he began turning heads.

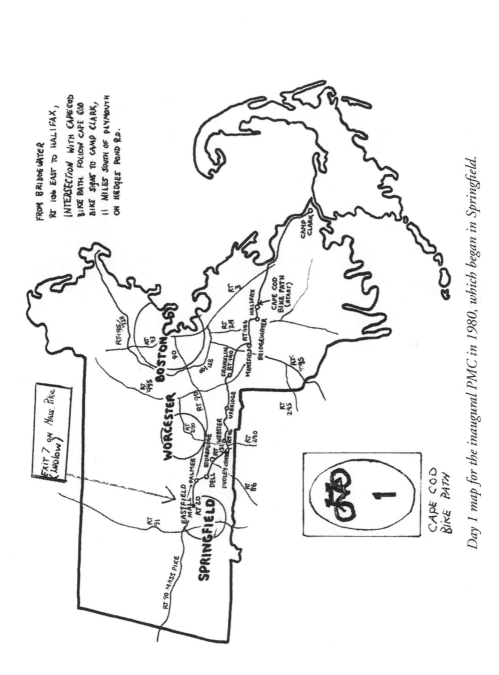

FROM BRIDGEWATER
RT 106 EAST TO HALIFAX,
INTERSECTION WITH CAPE COD
BIKE PATH. FOLLOW CAPE COD
BIKE SIGNS TO CAMP CLARK,
11 MILES SOUTH OF PLYMOUTH
ON HEDGES POND RD.

Day 1 map for the inaugural PMC in 1980, which began in Springfield.

Chapter Two

Creative Chaos

There was this great chaos Billy unleashed.

He and friends like Bresky and Chris McKeown were just getting their arms around it. With freedom to try new things, and make mistakes. One year their road coordinator obtained every address along the bike-a-thon route. McKeown, then Starr's right-hand man, had volunteers leave a purple balloon with a note in each mailbox, asking residents to tie one on during the weekend in support of the cause. "It was just this Zen thing," recalls longtime volunteer coordinator and rider Sue Brogan. "We saw them tied to mail boxes, tree limbs. Mostly we said to Chris, 'You are crazy. How did you come up with this?'"

"We were constantly trying to be different, something for every rider that's new, that's different," says McKeown. "And we were trying to get communities we traversed to embrace the PMC. Boy did we get in trouble with the postmasters. Who knew that putting anything but US Mail in a person's mailbox was illegal?"

A few days before the third ride Billy and Amy attempted to spray paint the entire route with arrows. They got into her truck and sparred much of the day, jumping in and out with the spray can. She wanted to put down more paint than he did. This took all day, and most of the paint wore off by the event. Another time her idea of placing name tags inside plastic covers utterly failed. By the first 20 miles the wind blew out the tags. "In those crazy years you're just trying to problem solve a thousand things at once," she says. "In those moments I just never felt more alive." Like a duck that appears to be gliding around with ease while little legs paddle mightily below the surface, volunteers worked furiously to get it done. At water stops Amy would be on her knees for two hours making peanut butter sandwiches as fast as possible. The immediate goal was always to improve the experience, which became one of the PMC's signature practices.

Those early years now feel like a far different era. Road biking in the early 80s was an up and coming niche, rough like the nascent enterprise of athletic fundraising itself. While nothing new in Europe, competitive biking, too, was about to take off among the masses in the states. The rock opera band Queen released "Bicycle Race" in 1978, after frontman Freddie Mercury was reportedly inspired by the Tour de France. The band produced a cheeky music video with models riding around Wimbledon Stadium in the buff. Here it was gym shorts or cutoffs, muscle tees and even sweats and wool shirts, no body-fitting spandex with chamois-lined crotch protection. Helmets weren't required. Whereas serious riders today may aspire to E6 Carbon Chamois bibs, in those days bibs then were meant only for babies. Your butt or groin usually chafed after a few hours. No one wore bike shoes except the hardcore. Few people had heard of a soy protein smoothie, and only pros sought out a nutritionist's help in a training vernacular of omega 3 fats, L-Glutamine and calorie schedules. Designer whey drinks were for aging hippies growing purple bud in Marin County.

Innovations naturally sprang up as new friendships formed, moving the PMC forward.

Meredith Beaton volunteered at her first event as a massage therapy coordinator in 1989 before she was dating Billy. An occupational therapist in Boston, she lured her physical therapist friends to help at the Massachusetts Maritime Academy. The campus along the Cape Cod Canal became the overnight stop and site of a refreshing afternoon party alongside the dock. Beaton and her friends all knew what to do, but they weren't prepared for the logistics. Riders dropped in all afternoon on to foam pads spread across the academy's ball field. Meredith and the others craned down working the riders' backs and shoulders at awkward angles for hours in the full sun. It was "the worst ergonomic set up you had ever seen," she says with a smile.

Someone handed Cindy Chase, another volunteer, a list of hundreds of riders waiting for a massage. Cindy figured there must be a better way. More than two decades later, she continues to tweak an appointment system and the setup for about 3,000 riders' massages, provided by 150 trained therapists who bring their own tables. Cindy organized 15-minute sessions with breaks for the therapists, and got it moved indoors. The ride-ending rubdown was so popular that it became a seminal goal for many. "They walk away and they can't even say 'Thank you.' They're in la- la land," Chase says. "Some say the last 20 miles all they think about is a massage." Cindy's system became a model for other events, such as the Boston Marathon.

Obstacles popped up as often as solutions, and volunteers or Starr's early fledgling staff always found a way around them. Local police at first resisted the gauntlet of riders coming through their towns. Some continue to complain, as Bourne's chief did in 2012, that the PMC is reluctant to pay for services it demands. McKeown remembers a chief in one community threaten he'd be at the town line with a shotgun. But with the Jimmy Fund's help, Billy set up a meeting with the police chiefs' association and took it from there. "We essentially co-opted law enforcement into accepting us," says McKeown. Today there's nary a major intersection that's not blocked off or patrolled.

While beginning to understand his own evolution, five years into it Starr didn't realize how vulnerable his dream actually was. He soon would. Thirty-five miles into the course what could have been a minor scrape led to the PMC's first fatality in 1984. By then the PMC was already growing into the largest contributing event to the Jimmy Fund, as some 366 riders would raise $155,000 that year. The morning was bright and dry when a 24-year-old rider named Michael Forbes flipped after hitting a soft sandy shoulder. He was wearing a leather helmet, but it did not prevent head injuries that later claimed his life. Billy rode up to the scene minutes after the accident. Forbes was in the ambulance, panicking, his limbs moving agitatedly. He went into a coma, and his parents decided to end life support the following day.

When Starr returned home that evening, the rider's voice was on his answering machine. Forbes had registered late, and said he looked forward to meeting Starr. Billy came undone, feeling the loss for the family. He also feared for the PMC. Badly shaken, Starr's core volunteer head staff quit. Along with Bresky and several others, Billy attended the wake where Forbes's father confronted him angrily. Yet the rider's brother stood by his side, trying to reassure Starr that it wasn't his fault. "It was a freaky thing and Billy said, 'I don't know what we could've done,'" recalls Karen Koshner, Starr's sister-in-law. In the end, the family seemed to embrace the spirit of what Michael Forbes set out to do, and left it alone.

Looking back on the accident, Starr considers it a marker of life's capricious nature. "If the tire rotated another three inches maybe he separates his shoulder. Instead, he loses his life." Billy doesn't agree, as people often submit, that it was "his time." Instead, he concurs there was no rhyme or reason. He calls it "the chaos theory," which first bit during his mom's 10-month illness. Hearing about the head injury, but not knowing the full implications yet, scores of riders heading home aboard the Provincetown ferry acted with intention, signing a card for Forbes.

The PMC was turning into a logistical and emotional mega event. By the 10th year ridership reached nearly 1,000 and donations to Dana-Farber easily topped $1 million. Starting ceremonies were moved from a small inn to the larger hotel in Sturbridge. A coordinator emerged for bike mechanics and the road crew expanded to nearly 100. Crowds gathered to cheer on the weekend warriors in small town centers like Uxbridge, which became legendary for their welcomes. A fourth hub would be added in addition to those in Sturbridge, Bourne and Provincetown, as shorter two-day and one-day routes took off from Babson College in Wellesley.

As interest in the bike-a-thon grew, whole families began to build their summers around the first August weekend. For many in the second generation, it's often hands-on problem solving and contributing to something very cool. Cindy Chase's clan from West Dover, Vermont, may be la familia PMC archetype.

Along with Cindy and her husband Jonathan, their children, Matt and Amanda, have been helping out, riding, or both, since 1987. Jon oversees merchandising and does the PMC's banking. He's a senior portfolio manager at Merrill Lynch. His first stint was procuring water bottles for a rest stop. Amanda, who finished college in 2011, is a summer intern and also rides with her dad. A little older, Matt helps run logistics including food distribution on the eve of the weekend. The Chase kids literally grew up in the PMC. Amanda was barely three months old, perhaps unknowingly soaking in orientation while her parents worked.

The family's weekend begins by setting up the merchandising area Thursday in Sturbridge, unpacking boxes of PMC jerseys, shorts and other riding gear. They break it down Friday night and ship whatever is left to Bourne. They fill in for each other until they're unloading gear and leftover food on the Monday-after back at the warehouse. Their parents' ethos, "You're never done, you're never done with the event," is inculcated in both young adults. As Matt told me one day at the warehouse, "Once you're in, you're in. There's no ever leaving."

"Everybody has their own reason for doing this but the one thing that's common is everybody wants to help to make a difference," Matt's father says. "Many of us are just blessed, knowing they can make it easier for someone else out there, helping them get through what they have to go through."

Like other volunteers, Cindy Chase continually strives for better. To further streamline the massage appointments, she'll bounce ideas off her daughter or the staff. "You take a deep breath and wait for it to start again," she says. Such sentiments are like fire-singed S'mores that the Chases and others pass around camp. "It's like a year didn't go by. You pick up where you left off," says Sue Brogan, another coordinator who is also a longtime rider. "I have people I only see on a PMC weekend and they are as dear to me as my closest neighbors. It's the best thing I do all year."

Among volunteers there's enough interest to hold a separate registration for alumni. Some 360 signed up the first day alone in 2012, many seeking back coveted jobs. By June, two months before the event, 128 crew leaders were gearing up for chores starting with salad preparation. To volunteer coordinator Sarah Mercurio, that's a mutually beneficial vibe among her charges and riders that doesn't fade away. A plethora of reasons exist that make people want to jump in: people directly affected by cancer, and those unable to fundraise who want to support the cause however they can. "For others," Mercurio points out, "it becomes part of their life."

As much as they pour out, at every level, participants receive much in return. A high school sophomore named Patrick in a maroon wool cap organizes kids at a Lego table as the Pedal Partner teams gather at a water stop. He has jumped in because a friend of his mother's has cancer. Lisa Martel, who lost her mom to breast cancer and has helped out for 15 years, rings a cowbell when a new rider registers in Sturbridge. It's a first step of her whirlwind weekend that involves serving breakfast, driving out to dish chowder beside the Cape Cod Canal, sleeping there in her truck, breakfast again at 4:30 a.m., home for a short nap on Sunday and then over to the start again handing out welcome-back snacks that evening. "It's reunion," she says after a novice signs in. "I come in and you see people once a year, but it's family. Anything to get rid of this crummy disease."

Starr addressing riders at the Provincetown Inn finish in 1988. For years afterwards, they paraded through town to the ferries chanting, "P-M-C."

Amy Bresky still shows up. Once she dressed as Carmen Miranda with a fruit basket on her head at a water stop beside a scraggly brickyard, where they dressed as hula dancers and filled an above-ground pool so riders could take a quick dip. While the dollars given to fight cancer are impressive, she's less interested in how the numbers themselves have ballooned. For Bresky the bottom line is this: "With so many horrible things people do to each other, over time it's really easy to forget about the good in people, and then you go to work with a group of volunteers and it all comes back to you."

In the mid-80s Starr met another rider who became his mentor and a close family friend. Even more, Sam Zoll occasionally reset the angle of Billy's rudder.

On the ferry home a 6-foot 6-inch rider approached Starr. He wore plaid pants with a sailor's cap atop a pink, bulbous face. "Eclectically horrible taste" in Billy's self-described "70s graduate's view." Zoll was a former mayor of Salem and chief justice of the Massachusetts District Courts at the time. It was his first PMC, he was impressed with the event and said he wanted to help. "I looked up at him and responded in classic Billy Starr diplomatese: 'That depends. Who the hell are you?'" Then Starr asked, "'Can you get me into the Mass. Maritime Academy? If you could, I could really grow this event.'"

Zoll shrugged his shoulders and said he'd look into it. "That fall, he persuaded Captain Arthur Desrocher (the academy's vice president) to allow the PMC on campus," Starr recalls. "But once Captain Desrocher began dealing with me instead of Sam, he quickly regretted his decision. When I would push Arthur's buttons over the next decade regarding expanding the PMC's campus imprint, he would vent to Sam about wanting to expel me and the event. Sam would then repave the road of good intentions with his velvet tongue."

The maritime academy provided a coveted midway respite on the way to Provincetown. Whereas they used to mainly tent at campgrounds near the canal, hundreds of riders began sleeping in dorms or aboard a training ship before a predawn reveille for day two. Other hurdles were soon overcome. Despite the best intentions, luggage distribution to dorms, tents and ship bunks resulted in many bags ending up in the wrong places. McKeown hatched an idea to get prerelease prisoners involved. He called his brother-in-law who worked in the state corrections department. Eventually, a system was devised. Working on the periphery of the event at the academy, low-security prisoners deliver luggage and later load bikes on trailers in Provincetown out in the ocean-fed air. Inmates also help set up lighting and logistics in Sturbridge.

A lasting dialogue ensued between Judge Zoll and Billy. Naturally, he sometimes joined Zoll's small North Shore riding group on Saturday mornings. Sam became a source of immeasurable strength, and a friend to Billy's dad as well. He advised the younger Starr on being an emerging public figure, how to handle the inevitable jealousies he would provoke, what to expect from a board exercising its powers, and the pitfalls of developing an organization. He presided over Billy and Meredith's wedding in 1991, which came just two weekends after the PMC, imploring her to be patient with her new husband.

Sam told them, "The lamp which you both carry in your life's work shines a bright light on the path of those who suffer and seek relief. It is a lamp that continuously shines preceding those on their search for a cure." Zoll urged them to be "thoughtful and give sensitive care and nurturing of each other should be your first and foremost priority."

Zoll also glimpsed the profound regard Milton Starr held for his son, and how living together many years after Betty's death became their lifeline. At times, Billy's papers and folders littered the dining room office. Yet they could both retreat to the den and watch a game, Milton perhaps deriding the Bruins for having too many men on the ice. His dad bought lunch, which helped Billy keep costs down. "But I also brought a vitality into that house that helped keep him alive," Starr says, recalling a nascent PMC beehive of volunteers during the spring and summer. It was reflected in the eyes of a man who nurtured the dream, even if sometimes on the sly. A friend of Milton's or a relative might ask, "When are you going to get a job?" Privately, Milton would continue talking up the PMC while Billy kept plugging away.

His support was a constant. He remained open, just as he and Betty had always opened their home to their sons' friends. It wasn't that he never had doubts. A worrier, Milton wasn't good at disguising his fears about liability, even well before the PMC's first fatality. At times he tried to put the brakes on his son's willfulness. But in the end, he was just very proud.

"It was a mitzvah," Yiddish for good deed, Billy says, "that I worked at home. And he lived to see it become an event of prestigious magnitude." Zoll shared this memory with a similar sentiment in a letter to Starr written shortly after his dad died at age 82 in 1998:

> *A discussion your Dad and I had some years ago. You were within view but not within earshot. It revolved around you completely. As he rotated his eyes from you to me, they had the glint of overwhelming pride, the words of both amazement and love and the tears of wonderful satisfaction that he desperately sought to hide. It was quite emotional, Billy, and I thought on that day how fortunate your relationship as father and son grew to reach such a special time and moment. You were both so very fortunate to have had each other.*

Samuel Zoll continued riding through 2009 and remained Starr's confidant, always one step ahead of his sometimes-celebrated protégé. Years later Billy would reflect, "I don't know how I can ever replace his wisdom but hope that his constant counsel to always be prudent and thoughtful has, at the very least, allowed me to approximate his superb judgment."

After ambling along for many years, the PMC's trajectory climbed rapidly beginning in the late 90s. Riders and donations grew from 1,715 participants (with 1,441 volunteers counted) raising $3.5 million in 1995 to almost 4,000 riders with 2,222 helpers raising $23 million a decade later. Earlier, Starr had hired a staff and his group of advisors formalized into a board of trustees. They pushed him further. This pickup emerged with the advent of online giving and opening up shorter, incremental riding routes. "That blew open the doors, going to multiple locations," says trustee Rob Smith. "From starting off with the endurance principle, which can be brutal to people, I think he realized the need to be more inclusive as riders aged."

The heady growth also certainly reflected an improving economy following the 1990–1991 recession. Volunteers, meanwhile, continued to leverage their connections to get deals from vendors, or kept pestering them as the new routes attracted more sponsors. It's a list with many endearing anecdotes, from landing Cape Cod Potato Chips to Fallon Ambulance. Starr kept stepping up his game. He became the consummate recruiter, landing big-name sponsors, and made sure he was involved in all facets of hiring and promotion. His zeal to grow the event coupled with a drive for efficiency that became legendary in the fundraising world.

Long before the term "intrapreneurship" was coined to denote a corporate culture that fosters innovation, the PMC was on the leading edge on the nonprofit side. Its practice of continuous improvement surges from the tone set by Starr. Skills honed during Billy's own outdoor experiences and recasting at his dad's table developed into a fiercely competitive operational style. David Fialkow, a longtime friend and rider who manages a venture capital firm, is another PMC trustee. "Phenomenal recognition skills," Fialkow begins, rattling off several of Starr's attributes. "Recognizing the riders, the givers and sponsors, making everybody feel very good. That's a strategy and skill and it also becomes a tactic. Lots of good communication and praise for people, for what they're doing. Second: phenomenal technology," including e-tools for credit cards and gifting, database analytics; how he registers riders, gets them into rooms, the use of mobile technology, the use of PR as a free tool. "It's all fantastic business acumen."

Fialkow can go on, and McKeown takes it another step back. Chris began riding in 1984 when he was still in the Navy, one of several siblings who cycled, while their mother and father and the rest of the family always volunteered. His clan became famous for its involvement. A volunteer needing help in the tumult leading up to the PMC might shout, "Someone grab me a McKeown!" Billy eventually pried Chris away from another career to be the PMC's first operations director in 1989, his first employee. McKeown's workspace began with a donated IBM computer in the bedroom of his basement. Alongside Starr he focused on growing the event and in a few years a friend of Billy's donated them office space. McKeown recalls that he week before the event was exhausting, but it was always worthwhile.

Chris credits early head staffers with building an organization whose hallmark became catering to the riders' needs. This clearly continues today, and McKeown suggests two of Starr's other strengths help key the growth: a tenacious drive and being a similarly voracious critical thinker. Those things sometimes rub people the wrong way, as Billy's occasional critics may equate the former with an inflated ego, but McKeown knows that's what many successful people require.

What began as creative chaos became an entrepreneurial contagion. Starr and his staff long pursued bringing every dollar raised by riders directly to the Jimmy Fund. "It became very important for him and the event," Rob Smith says. "The first goal was to get 90 cents of every dollar given, then 95, and then 100 cents...to the point where riders went to sponsors and told them there was no drag," or diversions of contributions to cover expenses. "Nobody is that efficient," Smith continues. "It happened because of his business model." Fialkow adds, "We on the board all marvel that he could be a brilliant CEO anywhere. He could run anything."

This mindset of continuous improvement seems ingrained in everyone who participates. People just keep stepping up. Charlie De Marco, whose family operates an Italian grocery in Malden, has lent out his trucks to help with the logistics for many years. He lost his father to cancer, and has been riding nearly two decades himself.

At a water stop in Lakeville, volunteer bike mechanic Alex Arapoff takes a quick break from patching tubes and replacing broken spokes. It's his fourth year helping out. His wife Susan is also riding again on a large team called Forza-G. While typical of many teams, the group's creative approach to fundraising blends many ingredients into a gastronomic delight: barbecue. Members smoke hundreds of pounds of pork shoulders annually and sell pulled-pork sandwiches at events like mountain bike rides across New England. Proceeds go into a pool to help team members reach their minimum and attract matching donations, Arapoff says.

Not far from him, riders are stepping in to a mist tent to cool down. Over three or four nights, Fred Reagan and Eddie Ennes built the tent with PVC tubing and 22 mist heads. "It's just a labor of love, it really is," says Ennes, whose doctor rides and inspired him to join in. "The gratitude I get. I should've started 10 years ago."

Jeff Rimpas, a volunteer head staffer who coordinates the Wellesley start, stays motivated partly by working with what he calls such a highly-functional team. "People don't just go through the motions," he says.

One of many volunteers helping out at a water stop in 2012.

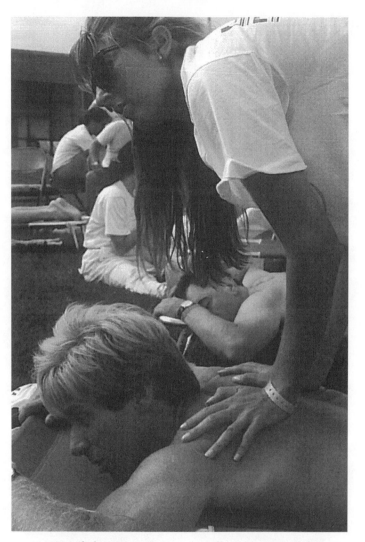

*Meredith Beaton Starr gives Billy a massage at the
Massachusetts Maritime Academy.*

"I don't hear, 'That's good enough.' When I'm riding, I'll often say, 'How long?' and 'What did you think?' They may say the food was okay or there was not enough. I do a little market research."

As with the riders, the loyalty of volunteers is fierce. Whatever attrition occurs is quickly replenished. Many of the core 18 or so "head staff" coordinators like Rimpas and another 100 so-called lieutenants, who devote extended hours throughout the year, are longtime veterans.

It's no accident that PMC volunteers like this inspire riders to reach new heights each year.

They eagerly correct any shortcomings and prepare to return. Some participating families even plan their vacations around PMC weekend. "It's like a wedding. You look forward to it all year long," says Cindy Chase. "The day after, you can't believe it's over."

All of which sustains and improves the riding experience. Along with typically great food, other perks are abundant: luggage delivery, omnipresent road crews, bikes transported home, ice chairs, ample hydrating, volunteers from every walk of life greeting you with a smile. A small band of riders even train in Italy with Starr during a spring tour. "Now it's like the Club Med of bike riding," says Nancy Tanner, who helps arrange some big sponsors including Stonyfield Farms yogurt, among other tasks. While there are many heartbreaking stories, she also observes the throngs stretching on the maritime academy grass in front of a band. "Some play volleyball," she says, "and you'd never know they just rode 100 miles." More than 70 percent of riders return the following year.

Always under the reunion tent there's this wiry camp director. A megaphone-waving carney barker, he's partly still a headstrong kid who goes off the trail thinking he knows a better way. But there's more to the job than that.

It's always been Starr's event, yet the PMC quickly grew into an extended family, obstinate and at times prickly, but reuniting with hugs and elation over a few cold beers at the end of a long day. While he may still come across as a my-way-or-the-highway guy, growing the bike-a-thon became more about inspiring others to keep raising the bar. Billy's drive no longer needed to be a model for the collective, because the collective kept reinventing itself. "He makes it easy for us because we don't have to worry about the vision," says Rimpas. "He communicates the vision consistently and unwaveringly so we know what we have to do. We don't have to worry about sponsors, we don't fret about that. All we have to do is improve it operationally."

One of Starr's ongoing joys is seeing all these people "vesting in something bigger than themselves. When you're one of 5,000 people, part of the quest, it's humbling and empowering, empowering to know there are people who think like you."

None of this can be considered accidental, despite the seeming randomness of certain traumatic events. The prefix "pan-" means "all", or using Starr's take on it, a "consensus of ideas." While he still relishes being the leader, Starr has never put himself far above the fold. "If people came to him and said, 'I have a great idea and I think we can do this better,' he was always, 'Great. Go do it,'" says Meredith, who has two daughters with Billy and a formal role in the PMC, assisting with stewardship and development. "He's always willing to trust people that they would make things better, and usually they do. But if they don't it's usually okay, if it wasn't a dangerous situation."

"He's not a micro-manager," she continues. "He lets people do what they feel they need to. And I think a lot of it comes from channeling grief. People are doing it for their own reasons and they're not paid."

As Meredith suggests, in one sense what Starr convened is a place and means for healing. He may be recalcitrant in that leadership role, his sacraments being his Trek bike, favorite jerseys and his final Wednesday night training ride. At times it's an undue burden, but it's part of his role nonetheless.

Explaining his thinking when he formed the event, Billy said, "It wasn't going to be about my mother, nor was I going to make myself a hero. I had learned that unless you buy in and take some responsibility, my leadership will be tempered by you doing whatever the hell you want. So I thought people had to have their own reasons for being there. I was going to create a box of rules and goals, but it wasn't about being there for my mother, and I've often counseled people who have benefits to memorialize a deceased child or a spouse. They've got to tell their story, but [participants] they've got to have their own story, they've got to have space for their own story."

Along with this role comes the difficult calculus of dealing with grief, both privately and sometimes publicly as the PMC's leader. Over the years Billy and Meredith have lost good friends, and two PMC riders in crashes.

They know full well the heartbreaks of many others who lose a loved one to disease. Both attend many funerals, where he's often asked to speak, and usually does. "It comes with the territory," she says. "It's part of the privilege of what he does, too, because he gets to know people in tough circumstances."

He's not callous at all, as people who've heard Billy's voice crack when offering an appreciation can attest to. Yet Starr isn't weighed down by the accumulated illnesses and losses. He admits he often cannot remember the types of cancer people have. "What's critical—and I suppose it's similar to a doctor's role or perspective—is it doesn't change my mission. It doesn't mean I'm insensitive, it just means it's not thatched to the center of my work—who had what particular form of cancer—as much as that I'm funding it." At times he pays tribute, but not under any compulsion.

Starr never seems to hit the proverbial wall. Yet he's had some close brushes.

In the early 1990s, by the end of one PMC weekend, as the event ramped up to nearly 1,500 riders, he got sick. Feeling overrun, he confided to Meredith, 'I've got to let some of this go.'" During those days Billy couldn't fully enjoy the ride itself. "If the hamburger rolls didn't show up, even if he was on his bike, he had to figure that out," she says. "There was no one else doing that."

There was also an emotional drain beyond those logistical challenges. "I don't mind when it's over now," he says. "In years past, I hated when it was over. I needed the reinforcement." Then in 2009, with another recession in full swing, for the first time in its history the PMC donation fell back from the previous year, down from a record $35 million to $30.4 million. Today Billy may downplay it, but Meredith knows he took it harder than anyone at Dana-Farber did. Not so much ego butting in as his drive.

"It's more that he feels—certainly it's his passion—but he's compelled that the money the PMC raises is so important," his wife says. It didn't take long for the riders and everyone else involved to get back up. The next year they climbed to $33 million. And they set their sights higher.

In 2000, Starr made another key hire, finally snagging his boyhood summer camp chum and hiking-cycling companion Dave Hellman. Dave is the one who stuck with him on the long, soggy Appalachian Trail. Hellman had managed IS systems and operations at ski resorts in Durango and Steamboat Springs, and run a department store chain. Starr had been grinding away at him for a decade, and when most of the store chain sold off, the time seemed right. Hellman had been back Wast to ride every August since 1990. "Because the event grew so much it looked like a different job when I took it," he says.

Back then almost none of the money came through credit cards. To cut down on delinquencies, which were at almost 20 percent, and process transactions smoothly, they began requiring riders to commit with a card before registering, a first in the industry. This commitment turns away some people, but for many others, it matches their passion. If a rider cancels, he still owes the money. There was some resistance, but Billy's stance is, "wanna-bees" need not apply. He has no tolerance for irresponsibility or welching. When early riders failed to meet their pledges, Starr's response was, "'You're screwing around with my event here,'" Rob Smith says. With Hellmann, the PMC staff rolled out other fundraising innovations. Among these were a self-guided system for tracking donations, publishing PMCers' stories, later on its thriving blog, and cutting check processing costs. "Billy's always figuring it out and he always will continue to figure it out," says Jimmy Fund Director Suzanne Fountain. "He's always on to the next technology."

Starr kept it a fundraising event from the get-go, not giving in to pressure against raising the minimum donations and requiring credit cards. Perhaps his most insatiable drive has been increasing corporate sponsorships, which is an off-stage production until their logos sprout up. For many years regional stalwarts like Stop & Shop and New Balance were in the fold. By 2011 John Hancock was aboard, BMW sponsored the maritime academy party and hosted a cool-down tent, and Billy landed Price Waterhouse Coopers to underwrite Sturbridge.

There were other gems. Among what Starr calls one of the three cornerstones of the PMC's dynamic growth was creating a shorter version "Boston start" from Wellesley in 1997, and landing an early media sponsorship with New England Cable News. Convincing the new Red Sox ownership to underwrite the PMC in 2003 topped them all.

Granted, Red Sox CEO Larry Lucchino didn't need a lot of convincing when Billy came to his office that winter. The new team owners were under pressure from the Secretary of the Commonwealth's office to give back mightily to the community through their charitable foundation. It was a no-brainer continuing the tradition of designating the Jimmy Fund as the official Red Sox charity. Starr asked them to step up as a PMC co-presenting sponsor. Lucchino had no qualms about underwriting operational costs. He had seen the event first-hand, and his wife Stacey, a future rider along with Tiffany Ortiz and other Sox wives, wanted to jump on board.

Larry is also a survivor of non-Hodgkin's lymphoma and underwent an experimental bone marrow transplant at Dana-Farber in 1986. More than that, his oncologist Dr. Lee Nadler was an unabashed PMC fan and had asked Lucchino to speak at its opening ceremonies, when Larry was still president of the San Diego Padres. When Lucchino met Starr at the opening in 1998 he immediately felt Billy's "energy and commitment, his energy, and his energy." His aplomb continues, "He is a force of nature and make no mistake about that. There is an old cliché that the great ones remind you of no one else, and I know of no one else like Billy Starr in terms of fundraising."

Starr didn't miss a beat as soon as he heard about the Henry-Werner-Lucchino group's bid for the Red Sox. "I literally started emailing my ridership saying, 'Let me tell you who you're rooting for. Because if this group wins, I've got to know I will be given an opportunity to pitch for the sponsorship support." He recalls his sales pitch to Larry as this: "You've got a public calling that you've got to give money. I'm already doing $15 million without you. What could I do with you?"

"I had tasted the spirit of the PMC so I knew it was a worthwhile endeavor, so we took it to our foundation board and they approved it unanimously," Lucchino says. Expanding the relationship with the Jimmy Fund included adding special PMC nights at Fenway Park, where the PMC logo is affixed to the iconic left field wall, and organizing the club's riders,

"Team 9," in honor of Ted Williams. For many years, Lucchino spoke at the Wellesley start beside Meredith. He could often be spotted cheerleading in Sandwich with his "Go Stacey" sign.

While he'll always be "from away," as New Englanders are apt to say, even to each other, Lucchino grasped another connection to the region. And to a larger purpose. "It's contagious," he says.

Chapter Three

Riding for Hannah

One day Sandy Fitzgerald was out walking with her amber-eyed granddaughter. She asked Hannah: "Do you think we'll ever take life for granted again?"

"Grandma, never," she said. "Never, ever."

When she was seven, right around Thanksgiving Hannah Hughes just wasn't herself. She was stuffed up and felt tired. A pain in her legs brought complaints, which was unusual. That Friday, when Sandy and her husband had Hannah and younger sister, Fiona, overnight, which is their tradition after the holiday, Hannah barely wanted to hang popcorn strings on the fresh Christmas tree. She'd recently asked Sandy to carry her bags in school. Her parents thought it might be a nagging sinus infection. Dark circles seemed to brood under her eyes, and her eyelids were a strange red. Hannah had black and blue marks all over. Tears rolled down her eyes as Hannah slept beside her grandmother.

When Jeff Hughes took his oldest child to the doctor the next Monday, they found an enlarged spleen and a white blood cell count that was through the roof. Her mom Rana was teaching a third grade class when the principal walked in. Your husband, he said, needs you to call.

Hannah was diagnosed with acute lymphoblastic leukemia. In just a few hours she was admitted to Albany Medical Center and began chemotherapy.

She has a rare genetic abnormality called the Philadelphia Chromosome-positive ALL. Having the chromosome makes one more susceptible to uncontrolled division of white blood cells that cause the disease. While not everyone with the Philadelphia Chromosome has positive ALL, children with positive ALL face an even higher risk of dying than those with some other forms of leukemia. She endured three rounds of treatments through that first winter. Then she underwent a successful bone marrow transplant with a donation from Fiona, who was five at the time. As Hannah's health inched forward there were months of near isolation, starting with 40 days in her room at Boston Children's Hospital, to avert any virus that might attack her depleted immune system. Then came a long rotation of check-ups with her oncologist close to home in upstate New York, and sometimes driving to the clinic at Dana-Farber.

Hannah endured other trials similar to what many children with cancer face: a grueling rotation of immunizations and intravenous antibiotics, cut off from friends and school life, all while facing the unknown. A knot still tightens within Jeff and Rana as they await a blood cell count, though not quite so taut as in those early months. At one time they dreaded any infection that might compromise her transfusion line. And putting in the double-lumen catheter line during that first week was harrowing. Their brown-haired daughter was emaciated at less than 50 pounds. The surgeon doubted he could do it, as Hannah's blood vessels were so tiny. He took off his mask, his face exhausted and creased. For an instant Rana thought the worst, the oncologist demanding, "You have to get it in." Twenty minutes took four hours. Yet the line held. "We owe him a huge debt of gratitude," her mom now declares.

For most of third grade Hannah was homeschooled. Play dates were limited, although her dad built a playhouse and they put a Porta-potty in the yard. It was safer to see friends outdoors because germs don't last long outside. She and classmates skyped during science lessons or to play a game of Hangman. On occasion Hannah attended school events, sitting outside the auditorium with doors opened, so she could listen in. She took a Chinese calligraphy class. But third grade wasn't easy, even returning to school for about two months to finish the year in 2012. "She says, 'I'm fine, I'm fine',"

Rana reported, "but after one and a half years of not being around kids, she's trying to find her niche. I knew there would be bumps in the road."

Her love of theatre helps smooth the potholes. Part of it is dressing up, whether as a gothic vampire or princess. Practicing lines with Fiona in the car, and taking a small role in *Wagon Wheel West*, Hannah regained her footing that spring. "She excels in that, her imagination," Grandma Sandy points out. Next door to their home in Ballston Spa, which is a small town at the foot of the Adirondacks near Saratoga Springs, a drama club practices three nights a week at the Malta Community Center. Both girls rehearsed for a production of *King Midas and the Palace of Gold* before the following Christmas, with their mom helping out back stage. Being in a cast of nearly 30, including several adults, made her feel so grown up. Even as a chorus member with only a few short lines. And Hannah was learning, Rana observed, how you must start at entry level and work hard.

While there are more benchmarks to clear, Hannah's flame continues to shine. A combination of treatments, including a targeted drug therapy, has—thankfully at least—halted, if not beaten back the disease. Still, as 2013 began, her parents were acutely aware of its possible reemergence just two years since the diagnosis. They remained vigilant of viruses, taking precautions to screen their once sun-splashed child, and of other more potent risks.

At times she seems beyond her years, taking in the whole world through those large eyes. Rana regards her daughter as a very old soul, her teammate since day one. She declares again, "That girl bounces back quick." In other moments, Hannah is in complete step with her peers, dancing to a Katy Perry song with her usual spunk in a skit that caps off a week-long run of "Girls Rule Camp." Swimming at the local pool again, she's likely to clomp up on the bus with her hair still wet and leave her suit on board.

Both Hannah and Fiona inspire many. Those who've long known Hannah marvel at her will to live. And others who've just recently connected with this family are lifted by something else, for Hannah is a giver who is apt to reach us all. At a young age, she already reaches out to others going through a similar illness, including a friend with Ewing's Sarcoma who had had her leg amputated. Another time, she found out about a mom from her school who was suffering from pancreatic cancer. Hannah told her

*Jeff and Rana Hughes flank Hannah holding
a Huckleberry bobble head outside the
Dana-Farber Cancer Institute in July, 2011.*

grandmother, who works as an aide there, "I know how she feels, and I'd really like to talk with her sometime." So the two of them sat knee to knee and talked.

Other remarkable things came Hannah's way. Neighbors and friends enveloped the Hugheses in those bursts of support that communities often muster. They held fundraisers at local restaurants and offered to watch Fiona. One woman ran a marathon, another started a website, "HotChocolateforHannah.com." For their own birthdays, Hannah's friends asked for money to send her in lieu of gifts, or gave up their own party to create one for her. Then her family joined an even bigger community, uniting with a PMC riding team that reinvigorated its purpose for her.

They call themselves the Huckleberries. And they added 184 miles of riding on the PMC weekend just to show up in her driveway.

On March 11, 2011, five-year-old Fiona, whom Hannah adoringly calls "Fifi," donated her bone marrow to give her sister a better chance of survival. It was their parents' second scariest day, sort of letting go control over both children. Jeff and Rana are firm believers in not hiding things from the kids, and told Fiona right away that her sister was ill. They didn't speak of leukemia or use the "c" word initially. Soon, though, the option of giving bone marrow came up and they had to try and describe that for their youngest.

"We basically explained that it comes out of her bone," Rana recalls. "We sat there in Boston and felt so stupid because we didn't know what it looked like. Did it come in a bag? We didn't know it looked like a blood product. We explained she would have a needle go into her back, which she equates with her hip, and marrow drawn out of each spot in her back and be brought to Hannah. They described it beautifully at the hospital. They said, 'You will give her a seed and she will have to water it and make it grow.'"

Fiona was nervous—about her sister being sick, and about her own role having surgery. Jeff and Rana were advised not to make it about "saving her" sister, just in case things went wrong. "It was one of those things where she asked, 'Is this going to hurt?'" her mom says. "We said, 'You'll be asleep,' and she said, 'I can do this. Yes.' It was kind of lumped together. And from there she sort of took on this ownership of wanting to be that helper."

"She still calls it her 'bone and arrow.'"

After the transplant Rana had trouble keeping it together. She went into the room and saw Fiona's puffy face, swollen from laying on her stomach during surgery. Yet her daughter sat up munching a huge green popsicle, oblivious to the two holes on either side of her spine. "She said, 'Mommy, Daddy, I didn't even feel it!'" as everyone including the nurses melted.

Hannah was isolated for 40 days after the transplant at Boston Children's Hospital, her mom staying there many nights and the family living in a nearby apartment. On a wipe-board calendar in her room, Hannah began recording two things every day with her mom: something I'm thankful for, and how I feel today. Thanks for Tylenol®; teachers who decorated their house before Christmas; for avocados, a new-found favorite; a camcorder;

her medicine; art supplies from Uncle John; Colleen, a nurse who put her at ease inserting an IV; and Natalie, a child-life specialist who helped her understand.

The couple were a close team often handling opposite ends of the ordeal. Whereas Rana focused on practical, day-to-day things and dealt with the surging emotional side, for months Jeff had gathered as much information as possible. When their doctor first told them about the Philadelphia Chromosome-positive childhood ALL, he couldn't believe she had it. Only about 100 children have this form of the disease among the roughly 2,000 kids diagnosed with ALL each year, and their chances for longevity are much lower. Essentially this condition occurs after a piece of one chromosome breaks off and switches places with another, activating a new gene that causes stem cells to overproduce far more than the body needs.

"I thought, there's no way that's what she has," Jeff recalls. "I would literally read and read and read and spend hours online, [looking for] anything on the process of what we needed to do to get her better." Early on Hannah was given a drug called Gleevec®, which had been first developed as a targeted or molecular therapy for chronic myelogenous leukemia. (Funding earmarked by PMCers also supported research and trials by a Dana-Farber team that led to the drug's approval for a life-threatening type of intestinal cancer.) While Gleevec®'s success blocking the single malfunctioning gene that causes CML is well documented, Jeff and Rana learned that clinical trials applying the drug for children with the Philadelphia Chromosome-positive ALL were quite recent. It worked well enough lowering Hannah's cell counts for her doctors to recommend moving ahead promptly with the transplant. Her timing was fortuitous. If she had been diagnosed two years earlier, at best she would have been part of a study. "I feel by being able to take it daily she was in some good shape before the transplant," her dad says.

After the transplant Hannah passed through other dangerous waters. As Jeff explains, "all sorts of issues," including fungal infections, the possibility of seizures, kidney and liver damage. "Any infection itself can be the end of the process. That's what makes Dana-Farber great. They know about this and are great about managing the process." Jeff continued both his studies and his job as a salesman for a wine and spirits distributor, for which Hughes puts on a lot of miles. Fiona bounced back quickly. While she was anemic and needed giant doses of iron, their daughter soon resumed bouncing around the apartment and returned home with her dad. Hannah, Rana and Sandy then relocated to the family's 30-foot camper for a month. Driving it to a campground in the Boston suburbs, they were close enough to get back to the hospital as needed.

The hospital staff was concerned that living in an RV would compromise her recovery. But Jeff, Rana and her mother shampooed the rugs and scrubbed it clean to set up a controlled environment. A space of their own, with mother and daughter cozying up and usually sleeping together. Sandy sometimes sat on one couch and Hannah on another watching the Disney Channel. "She was so fragile," Rana recalls. "I was doing the flushing and hooking her up to an IV; it was like having a newborn." Through the draining treatments, which also included radiation, and beginning long months of isolation they were a team again, her daughter "so good at listening and reminding me of things." In many ways, her miraculous firstborn, who'd arrived late and always did things on own her time, would continue to point the way. "I cannot, for one second, use any of this time with Hannah to feel sorry for myself," Rana journaled. "She doesn't do it so why should I? Each day I have with my girls is a gift."

The day Hannah underwent the transplant, Alex Smith, a young woman who enjoys playing with kids, introduced herself to the family in the Jimmy Fund Clinic waiting room. When she's around children, Alex's wide smile forms dimpled cheeks and you're likely to find her wearing a plastic crown or a silly hat. Smith coordinates a PMC program called Pedal Partners bringing together children and teens in oncology with riding teams. The idea, she says, is to connect a group of PMCers who carry bigger-than-average hearts with families of a similar makeup, who often offer something in return even in moments when they feel as if they don't have much left.

Alex didn't need to attempt a hard sell with Rana and Jeff. But their heads were spinning. Rounds of intensive chemotherapy had just recently ended, while Rana had taken a leave of absence from teaching. Jeff recalls Smith's approach. "We're sitting there and after you get the gloom and doom of what this may be entailing. It was a question as to whether you'd even make it out after 30 days." She told them about the PMC and pointed out some posters and information. They had no idea what the event was. Rana was more inclined to do it, while her husband thought it was a bit crazy at the time. "I'm a firm believer and hopefully show my kids that if something like this happens, if there's a way to help other people, we should try," she says. If left up to him, Jeff admits he probably would have said, "'No thank you,' but Rana having been the one always looking to be involved and active. We were like, whatever, sure." Hannah agreed to be a riding team partner and they took her picture.

Smith had just the cycling team in mind: The Huckleberries.

They are named for a now-defunct bakery in western Massachusetts, whose owner had a beagle, itself the namesake of the pale blue, often befuddled Hanna-Barbera cartoon hound. The one with a southern drawl that had a way of stumbling upon the resolution of each episode. Which all sounds kind of Hostessy-sweet.

Two riders, Dave Grossman and Jonathan Siegel, made a first stop at Huckleberry's Bakery & Cafe in 1997. That was the first year they decided to start the PMC a day early from the New York border in order to make it truly "pan-Mass." Doing so added one day and about 100 miles to the traditional Sturbridge start, not a big deal for serious riders like Dave and Jon. They started through the Berkshires on Route 20 and found the diner-bakery about 35 miles in for their first break. "We got such a kick out of the place. It became our traditional stop because it had fantastic muffins," says Grossman. As they formed a team the name stuck. Perhaps like the doughy muffins, which some other Hucks detested—along with the establishment's reputed tepid, watery coffee, and gnarled waitstaff. But that's another story, perhaps a very minor sticking point, for later.

By 2011 the Hucks had long been riding for relatives, and a few even for themselves and their spouses. They never needed another reason to ride, yet they still yearned to sponsor someone new. Among the many PMC veterans, their core group of 14 riders had more than 400 years doing the event between them. On his seat back Grossman carries names including those of his mom, his mother-in-law and maybe a dozen others. It's similar for many of his mates. He contacted Alex Smith that spring hoping to match up with a young patient.

Smith thought pairing Hannah and the Hucks might work. She figured that in the event Hannah was too sick to venture far in August, at least the team could meet somewhere close to her home, perhaps along the New York border. Grossman contacted Rana and read about Hannah in a CaringBridge online journal that her mom maintains. He googled Ballston Spa, Hannah's hometown, and then emailed the team: "Guess where you're starting this year." Dave knew that at minimum, his group could help lift them even momentarily. "What I didn't realize is how much she gave back to us, just the family's strength," he says.

Team Huckleberry got in motion early. Each member introduced himself or herself in a book with short profiles and photos: Steve from New Jersey, whose Maltese puppy brings his cycling shoes to the front door when he's away; Scott, a chip designer at Intel with three kids; Ellen, the California "Huck chick" riding her 7th PMC; Remy, a computer programmer whose company helps scientists find cures; Tim, a longtime rider whose wife and brother are both cancer survivors; Joel, a scientist at Pfizer, a former amateur racer and survivor of Hodgkin's lymphoma; and Jon, whose wife beat breast cancer and who has two kids, three cats, and a lizard named Sebastian.

What had once been a spirited two-day ride would become four, with strenuous climbing added in the Taconic Crest along the state border. Ellen Kirk, who typically flies in from her San Diego home or from a business trip to Boston a few days before the PMC, could already anticipate a savored reunion with friends. Joined at the hip for a few days, partying hard at night—and then encore disparu save email until the next season. "Nothing," she says, "gets to take over that weekend." And perhaps nothing could prepare Kirk for how a sister's bond, little Fiona's choice, would impact her.

When Grossman and his wife first met Rana and Hannah that May at Dana-Farber, they brought Hannah baskets with art supplies she loves. She was covered head to toe by a surgical mask, an oversized sweatshirt, and a Red Sox cap, to protect her compromised immune system. She handed Dave a card thanking the team for being her partner along with $75 of her own money. Dave split it with his teammates, already feeling his experience was being redefined by a little one who was just getting started. This would be his 30th ride, so he already knew full well the energy of PMC weekend. "You just have to look around you, and it hits you right in the gut," he'd offer later. Yet connecting with Hannah meant something more.

The Huckleberries had an official team jersey designed, and into the summer Grossman stayed in contact with Rana and her family. He kept the team informed of Hannah's progress. "I said, guys, we're making a difference here, and we're like direct beneficiaries of this now." Upon learning that her favorite color is purple, he brought Hannah an aptly hued mortarboard and wrote her signature expression on it, "Make the Best of Every Day." Fresh from his own son's college commencement, Grossman went a step further. He envisioned Hannah graduating—from Dana-Farber. He vowed, "She's getting a purple gown."

He wrote a note that he hoped she could open the following summer:

> *You have navigated your way through very difficult obstacles, always with incredible bravery and confidence, displaying a commitment and maturity beyond your years, because you knew that you would beat cancer.*
>
> *Hannah, you have been an inspiration to all of us. You have always viewed the world as "half-full" despite all the challenges put before you, and you truly believe in the philosophy that everyone should "Make the Best of Every Day."*

For Hannah and her family, spring into summer was a fragile if not sometimes perilous stretch, with occasional rays of light. Her body could not produce enough antibodies so she was essentially quarantined when indoors. She got out for short spurts with friends. Jeff and Rana guarded her from the sun, which before her diagnosis would turn her dark hair nearly blonde. They learned that radiation treatments ratchet the risk for skin cancers. Some three months after her transplant they had a nasty scare. A test for the chromosome that caused her leukemia was positive, apparently a false positive. They were temporarily devastated, Jeff says, because a positive result at that stage meant it was near certain that the cancer would return. But they found out that someone had given the wrong test. Upon redoing it, there was no threatening trace.

Her grandfather, Garry Fitzgerald, refurbished his screened-in porch with new furniture and a heater so she could visit outside. Sandy had promised Hannah art lessons and arranged for a teacher to paint with her outside, with gloves on in the chill.

In June Hannah joined a community workshop—greeting classmates and others outside—for a charity that encourages children to create art that's used to design bed sheets, room dividers, and other things that brighten up a hospital for others. The Kidz b Kidz founder had brought her art supplies to Boston, and Hannah went to work drawing a lion that was used later to design hospital johnnies. The next month, she sat in the back of her dad's pickup as the "honored hero" watching a 5K benefit run and walk at a state park for other cancer patients.

Both Hannah and her parents would reciprocate in kind. A few months later Rana reflected on the unexpected ways new people were crossing their path:

People come into your life for a reason, a season or a lifetime. When you know which one it is, you will know what to do for that person. When someone is in your life for a REASON, it is usually to meet a need you have expressed. They have come to assist you through a difficulty, to provide you with guidance and support, to aid you physically, emotionally or spiritually ...

Some people come into your life for a SEASON, because your turn has come to share, grow or learn. They bring you an experience of peace or make you laugh. They may teach you something you have never done. They usually give you an unbelievable amount of joy. Believe it, it is real. But only for a season!

A new season unfolded. The Hucks were coming. That August, a contingent of what Starr casually dubs the psychic well-being club would cross her driveway in the form of 13 riders.

Chapter Four

A Line Walking Together

A t least once a year Bill Hahn can enjoy his anonymity. Most of the time, he is a genitourinary oncologist and chief scientific officer directing the Center for Cancer Genome Discovery at Dana-Farber. Then for two days, he's just one of the herd again.

A crop of thick black hair and his broad face are bunched in under a helmet. He soaks it all in. The outpouring of gratitude, so intense as to almost make him a little

Dr. William Hahn

uncomfortable, never wanes in its effect on Dr. Hahn. It builds during his spring training rides, supplemented by feedback he receives from sponsors, and people at the hospital and everywhere thanking him beforehand and after.

He wants to give a shout-out to everyone else. He's seen the risks that Dana-Farber has been able to take, such as acquiring gene-scanning equipment and providing lab space to further genomic research. This began in the late 90s, and more recent discoveries are transforming "the whole vision of cancer therapy," one of Hahn's colleagues notes. In just one example of their pursuits, advances in gene-sequencing technology enable researchers to quickly spot gene abnormalities in tumor tissue, and even rank those genes that are the most likely suspects contributing to cancer.

"You don't think you deserve so much praise and thanks, because I mainly ride to honor the patients I've had," he says. "I feel like I should be thanking the people who are thanking me. They are the ones working all the rest stops, behind the scenes making the work possible. It's an amazing accomplishment what they do, thousands of people standing by the side of the road cheering on a bunch of people they don't event know, and there are a hundred other things they could be doing. It's just amazing."

"They're taking time out to do something, it's very different," Hahn says. "Its harder to explain why they're doing that than why you're riding the bike. It's easy to explain why you're riding the bike."

At multiple and far-reaching levels, the bike-a-thon supports the some-times magical work that Hahn and others have long been doing at DFCI. Medical breakthroughs have become the norm at Dana-Farber and its predecessors ever since Dr. Sidney Farber began his research in a poorly ventilated chemist's closet at Children's Hospital. In the summer of 1947, the pathologist set his focus on childhood leukemia, reasoning that that since it could be measured in the blood, any chemical intervention could also be evaluated. By the next winter, Farber tested the first chemother-apy to temporarily halt progression of that disease, injecting a synthetic antifolate into a two-year-old named Robert Sandler, whose white cell count stopped climbing. The research center Farber established grew as successive leaders recruited some of the world's best physician-scientists and built facilities for inpatient and outpatient care. Through the 1970s, what was then known as the Sidney Farber Cancer Institute began racking up research achievements, including pioneering the use of multiple drugs, and increasing cure rates for several diseases. They were just scratching the surface.

Decades later, as Boston's Longwood medical district continued to expand, collaboration among Dana-Farber and other teaching affiliates of Harvard Medical School reached new heights. The array of discoveries and quality of patient care that often results can give us all pause. In 2011 alone, the Dana-Farber/Harvard Cancer Center—a consortium including six other Harvard-affiliated institutions—conducted nearly 700 clinical trials, collectively one of the most robust programs anywhere in the world. Dana-Farber saw more than 353,000 outpatient clinic visits and infusions by children and adults. Among its areas of expertise, DFCI together with Boston Children's Hospital remains top-ranked for pediatric and blood disease programs and with Brigham and Women's Hospital, is one of the country's top cancer hospitals for adults.

In a perennial nod to the contributions of Starr and his legions of participants, Dr. Edward Benz, Dana-Farber's CEO, often offers that when the book gets published on how a cure for cancer was found, the PMC will be the first chapter. While there may be a slice of hometown boosterism in that prediction, the Pan-Mass is no less a critical spark plug in the crusade.

Often enough, Dr. Lisa Diller sees this marvel close up. She is the Chief Medical Officer of Dana-Farber/Children's Hospital Cancer Center, the integrated cancer center and pediatric hospital. A pediatric oncologist, clinical director, researcher, she is also a mom, and much more. Diller says when people like the Hugheses come in, "At first when I get the call my heart goes out for the family, it's so hard. But then my heart soars because they've found the right place, the right team."

"It's a very expensive special sauce," she told PMCers in 2011, referring to that chemistry of institutional risk-taking and caregiving. "And thanks so much for raising the money that helps us bring the special sauce." Their gifts positively impact a bottom line that cannot just be read in the financial statements. For Dr. Diller, this means developing "smarter therapies that target the disease and not the patients. That what the labs are working on, that's what the scientists are working on, and that's where the clinical trials are."

Jothy Rosenberg is indefatigable. Starr once said, "Stick is what it's about," explaining that the PMC's clout stems from how people make the ride part of their lives. Rosenberg embodies a complete attachment few of us can fully grasp. He and his supporters keep stirring the sauce that Diller's patients and colleagues so need.

A teenage cancer survivor and disabled athlete, Rosenberg's motto has long been, "Who says I can't?" His blog, a book and a reality TV show amplify this theme. He beat osteogenic sarcoma but not before his right leg had to be amputated. And when the cancer metastasized three years later, two-fifths of his lungs were removed. Dana-Farber developed the chemotherapy given to him in 1976, which, he says, "is the only reason I'm still around."

Rosenberg rides the full route with just his left leg. "I don't know how my leg can do it, but I keep telling my leg to do it, and come one way or another, my leg is able to push and pull for 192 miles," he says. "That is just a reflection of 'I'm going to conquer this thing.'" He and his wife Carole formed a riding team that brings in enough money to fund a top researcher devoted to osteosarcoma, Dr. Katherine Janeway, who is also an assistant professor of pediatrics at Harvard Medical School. It's a relationship Rosenberg believes is unique in that field. He doesn't need additional motivation. While osteosarcoma affects only about 1,000 kids in the U.S., "it's a bad one," he says. "That kid who has to have a fibula or tibia replaced and can no longer can play sports, or gets an amputation and must play it differently." The rupture to self-image requires ongoing tending.

When he rides, Rosenberg carries other remembrances. In 2011 he met a young woman, Stirling Winder, then 25, near the beer tent at the maritime academy. She was studying to be a pediatric nurse practitioner. But Stirling had a replacement knee and the same cancer was spreading to her other organs. An athlete who'd played Division 1 field hockey in high school, she rode the PMC once, and died a year after meeting Jothy. "I wish I got to know her better," he blogged. "I am so sorry she is gone now."

He does grueling fundraisers like the Sharkfest swim to Alcatraz, 375-mile AIDS rides, and other bike-a-thons. He was never a superstar athlete as a kid. And while slightly pudgy these days approaching 57 years, Rosenberg also continues to do what one doctor forecasted he wouldn't be able to do again when he was 19: ski. Not just those trails that are a mere Starbucks' Venti-length ride away from his home in Newton. On major mountains out West like Alta and Jackson Hole. Back then, Jothy took off and literally logged 100 straight days skiing black diamond slopes. Sometimes he asks himself, "Could I have done these things if I had *not* got cancer and an amputation in my teenage years? We will never know. One of these days I will figure it out."

The PMC somehow ups the ante. Even though Rosenberg is a widely successful entrepreneur with eight startups to his credit, he still battles what he describes as a constant downward push on self-esteem. "To the outside world, it looks like he's figured out how to walk with one leg, he's all set, all done—and that is not true. You are reminded all day, every day, that something's different. For me it happens if I walk too far, the plastic against my skin hurts, or if walking up a hill or a ramp, the knee stops working, you get a stiff leg, so you feel like a gimp. Every person is reminded of it every day."

"I love passing two-leggers on that ride," he continues. "It is the biggest ego-booster you can imagine. I pass hundreds and they all say good things. And I just rode to raise money for the type of cancer and research that saved my life. That's three, huge, friggin' things."

While its support for Dana-Farber is momentous, the PMC's footprint and legacy may even be bigger.

The nonprofit is the leader of a $4–5 billion "thon" industry raising money for charitable causes in the United States. While some may see its monetary contribution as the bottom line, there are other elements in play which make the PMC a legacy-setter. There's a relentless drive to land both corporate sponsors and in-kind contributors, who serve up $5 million in goods and services each year. While the term "value-added" may have become cliché, many of those sponsors actually refresh this concept by encouraging employees to participate and by integrating such fundraisers into their corporate culture. Both volunteers and riders step outside of themselves in high levels of participation. "It's a story that, as much as it's been told, it still hasn't been told enough," offers Mike Dee, a PMC rider and trustee.

When it comes to athletic fundraising, the PMC simply sets the bar. Since 2007 it has achieved a 100 percent pass-through rate to DFCI, which is the envy of any nonprofit. Led by Starr's insistence, and infused by his staff and the trustees, the organization has remained lean and true to its entrepreneurial roots. For many years there were only seven paid employees. Fixed expenses including salaries are covered by corporate underwriting, registration and merchandising. Hoping to sustain its growth, heading into 2013 the organization was finally adding new positions including a director of sponsorship and donor development, and a finance and administration chief.

David Hessekiel is president of the Run Walk Ride Fundraising Council, an industry group that tracks athletic fundraising. While he hasn't yet met Starr, the PMC's reputation precedes him. "There are other programs, but none of them come close to its range, nor the sense of attracting business sponsorship to cover the logistical and administrative costs," says Hessekiel. "Those are all primary positions, and having the hometown popularity, and being able to state every dollar you raise goes to Dana-Farber, all of that is very powerful."

"As a trailblazer, they have imitators," he says. "Not copycats."

The event inspires others in the cause, and Starr occasionally is called for advice. He gave an early assist to the fast-growing Pelotonia Ride in Columbus, Ohio, which raised $42 million for cancer in its first four years, and to similar events in St. Louis, Tampa, and Toronto. The PMC has a direct line to the Dolphins Cycling Challenge, which rallies support and trains the public spotlight on the University of Miami's Sylvester Comprehensive Cancer Center.

Soon after arriving in Miami in 2008, new Dolphins CEO Mike Dee set one of his sights beyond Sun Life Stadium. Dee's relationship with the PMC began when he was Red Sox COO under Larry Lucchino. Joining the Sox's Team 9 for the PMC became an annual rite of passage. He still marvels at memories of riders waking up at 3:30 a.m. on day two, hanging out beside the Cape Cod Canal, and his signature moment crossing the bridge at daybreak.

When he came to Miami, he discovered the Dolphins' and Hurricanes' interest in looking at other ways to complement each other beyond sharing the stadium. Dee learned that some people felt the Sylvester cancer center was undervalued in the area. "This idea was always in the back of my mind, what could we do with the bike-a-thon," he says. "Not necessarily mess with Sylvester's DNA—they are already great—it was more to see what we could do to make Sylvester more prominent in our community and have more of an impact." The hospital wanted to expand satellite facilities and attract more researchers. Billy and his number two guy, Dave Hellman, went down and gave operational and fundraising tips. "To think of doing anything that would be like the PMC would be a daunting task," Dee says. "It's such a well-oiled machine, and every year it drives out farther. You do not try to replicate it."

Three events later, some 2,000 riders raised $2.2 million in 2012, setting a single-event record for an NFL team's donation. The Dolphins' challenge was growing by leaps and bounds, up from some 800 riders the previous year, for a combined $3.8 million contribution. It's already become unique to Dee. Starting at the stadium, the route immediately cuts through a blighted area with some tough neighborhoods in the first 40 city miles. "And people are out in the street cheering us on, saying, 'Go Dolphins' and 'Keep riding,'" he says. "We finish in Palm Beach where there are $25 million-dollar home neighborhoods. That's interesting in itself because you know the chances of cancer affecting an individual is random, and just as great for either."

"The economy is not ideal," he continues, "but I think the greater downside for us and any fledgling event getting off the ground is how do you put the institution and the cause at the center of the message? I've got to believe if all South Floridians believe at some point they will be impacted, and the numbers confirm this, then everyone would want a cancer facility to be there in their footprint when that event takes place."

There are, of course, much larger multi-event athletic fundraisers than the PMC. Coupled with untold local ones, they form a distinctive patchwork in the quilt of American charity. Walks for causes from Alzheimer's to breast cancer seem to be everywhere. By one accounting, some 11.6 million Americans in 30 top-generating programs increased their contributions 2.5 percent in 2011 despite a tough economy. (The PMC was ranked 16th overall when the multi-event nonprofits are included.) Some three million people do 5,000 Relay for Life events, the largest combination of these fundraisers, which raise $415 million for the American Cancer Society. These events range from round-the-clock walking in Agoura Hills, California, to a Mardi Gras-themed Run for Life in Indiana, to dancing in a Moultrie, Georgia, courthouse square. There are even longer cycling events, such as the 545-mile AIDS/Life Cycle ride down the coast to Los Angeles.

The feel-good-by-doing movement has come a long ways since the country's first March of Dimes walks in the 1930s, or a noted inaugural walk-a-thon by churchgoers in Bismarck, North Dakota, for hunger programs in 1969. On nearly any given weekend, creativity runs in gorilla suits or Santa speedos. There are open-water swims, turkey trots, and neighbors circling their high school tracks. Extreme athleticism and casual strolls have become synonymous with giving back.

Yet there may not be anything quite like the PMC. That moment in the cemetery each summer seals it for Ellen Kirk, one of the Huckleberries riding for Hannah. She's in a group that becomes virtually inseparable for four days, sharing stories "of people close to us who are either battling cancer or whom we've lost recently," she says. "And it's like weaving again another layer of complexity."

Our family has a connection of its own. My mother Joan underwent two years of treatments and surgeries for ovarian cancer in the late 1990s at Brigham and Women's Hospital, just up the street from Dana-Farber. She was under the care of Dr. Ursula Matulonis, a soft-spoken oncologist who went the extra mile and was always clear. My mother's life ended about two weeks before her 60th birthday in 1999. Today Dr. Matulonis directs the Gynecological Oncology Program at Dana-Farber's Susan F. Smith

Center for Women's Cancers. Primarily through my father's drive, and the generous contributions of employees at the company he devoted 52 years of his life to building, we continue to support the work of her program.

Ursula and her team are dogged and caring. As years progress they chase down increasingly promising leads. One project continuing into 2013 has to do with profiling the different mutations in oncogenes, those genes with the potential to cause cancer. The study, which began in 2010, is a part-

Dr. Ursula Matulonis

nership between Dana-Farber and Brigham and Women's that amounts to what she calls a personalized medicine program for ovarian cancer. By honing in on the different mutations, Matulonis and other investigators probe for "Achilles' heel" defects that make particular gynecologic cancers susceptible to certain targeted therapies. "We've been able to identify several mutations that could be important in treating ovarian cancer since drugs that target these mutations are currently being tested in clinical trials," she wrote. Going further, her group is expanding its "genetic interrogation" of ovarian cancer, such as testing whether there are too many of certain genes or whether some have been deleted.

Matulonis often finds time to explain the work of these teams. In the fall of 2012 there were eight open clinical studies underway, whereas 15 clinical trials had been completed in recent years. New drugs were being tested to accomplish things such as blocking signaling pathways within a cancer cell. These include agents that block new blood vessel growth (i.e., anti-angiogenic agents), medications that interfere with the repair of DNA in a cancer cell called PARP inhibitors (i.e., olaparib), and drugs that block signaling pathways inside the cancer cell such as PI3kinase inhibitors, she said.

Once drugs are tested by themselves and found to be promising, they are then tested against a standard of care therapy, Matulonis continued. "Our group is now running four such studies, three of which are led by DFCI investigators. These agents include: MM121, which blocks a protein called HER3, which is felt to be important in ovarian cancer; Cabozantinib (XL184), which blocks 2 proteins called VEGFR2 (important for angiogenesis) and c-MET (important for a cancer cell's ability to invade); olaparib, which is a very active PARP inhibitor; and MLN8237 which is an aurora kinase inhibitor.

"Our group has also started rationally combining different targeted drugs such as olaparib and cediranib in order to overcome resistance the cancer cell might have to a certain class of drug. Another phase one study led by a DFCI investigator that is run through our Stand Up to Cancer team is combining a PI3kinase inhibitor and a PARP inhibitor for women with high-grade serous ovarian cancer, the type of ovarian cancer that is most common." Coupled with other discoveries at the Smith Center and elsewhere, the advancements ripple out.

Meanwhile, Matulonis's clinical group kept pace as one of the country's busiest, seeing 200 newly diagnosed ovarian cancer patients a year. The team of medical oncologists, gynecologic oncology surgeons, radiation oncologists, along with nurse practitioners, program nurses, and a physician assistant handle more than 12,000 outpatient visits annually. All of which requires supersized coolers full of backing to sustain. Among the many other teams and disciplines, the Gynecological Oncology Program attracts substantial support. In 2011 alone, several new contributors stepped up for women's cancer research including New England Patriots' owner Robert Kraft and his sons, in memory of his wife and their mother, Myra Kraft. They selected Dr. Matulonis to direct their fund.

It's all heady stuff. That is, if you have the intellectual wherewithal, and perhaps the emotional fortitude, to process this. When my mom was sick, most of the time I didn't.

I could only vaguely grasp her prognosis or any technical detail. A foggy wall stood between medical realities, its instrumentation, and what my gut was telling me. A shared intuitive love and trust in who I was becoming had always emanated from her. So I followed that again. Pretending not to need all the details. Her TPN and double port were as foreign to me as concepts like inhibitors and germline mutation. At the very end, she didn't need to tell me she loved me. I accepted her loss just as I'd always believed in her.

One unusually warm day in early December, some 13 years later I asked my dad a little about that time. We sat in their house overlooking a harbor on Buzzards Bay, the water barely moving, a few small black and white bufflehead ducks making their way near the shore. A lone workboat was out attaching the last winter sticks to some mooring tackle.

It was the kind of day my mother appreciated in full. There was something about Joan, he said, that seemed to attract both Ursula and her oncology social worker to her. Both women drove out to see her for a last visit about a week before she died. "I think they had a great deal of respect for how she handled her illness," my father said. "While she was devastated, she handled it the best she could." My mother was a special education teacher and vocational counselor, a caregiver, and our glue, a longtime choir member who finally took up jazz piano adding to her repertoire of show tunes, carols and children's singalongs. Imperfect, depressed at times, she came from old, complicated New England stock, Haskells and Carles. Her dad grew up on the Merrimack River. The son of a truck farmer, and never wanting to farm himself, he worked many years as a haberdasher and salesman, something always eluding him.

There were many moments of grace. She was the one who made that second phone call you came to expect, maybe an hour after a difficult conversation, apologetic: "I hope I didn't overstep..." Or to mend a family rift: "I think it would be a good thing if you called..." She was the one each of our kids and their younger cousins flocked to, because while gently plying their curly hair on the couch or up on her bed, she'd tell them a snarly story. She was the one who, with help from some dear friends and a cousin, made scrapbooks for our three children in her hospital room. I'll never forget the night Nana Joanie and Grampa Bobo gave those books to them, and it was only weeks away. She was the one who brought in so many friends, in moments listening to their own misplaced needs, to ease their grief.

In those last few months, as the waning late fall light continued warming their living room, my dad was often chief nurse, checking her morphine drip and TPN and cleaning the drain. He knew that she shared so much of her illness because her mother had not. Virginia was taken by the same disease far too early, during Joan's junior year at a teacher's college. Her mother stayed in bed and kept it to herself.

A few years after my mother died, I found this poem she had written for Virginia in 1995. One day when the wind was "stirring up the grasses," she scrawled it in a journal kept at our family camp in Maine.

How I wanted to know you better – and have you come to know and understand me.
I needed you to help me find my way … I have found this journey hard at times –
And felt the bumps – While I smelled the sweetness of the rose – embracing the soft air.
For I have loved with all the passion of my soul.
I've missed you more than I have let myself know.
Today I see so clearly that you are here – Planted deep in my memory –
The sweetness of your smile, the sparkle of your pale, blue eyes –
Your gentle laughter, your quiet ways – The integrity of your soul.
You taught me about strength – the courage to endure and transcend the struggles of our lives –
How to walk in a woman's quest for wholeness.
The light is clearer now – Here in this place –
Touched by the softness of the morning sun, the deep purple hues of the evening sunset I've come to see and know myself
As part of this legacy, this heritage of respect for all that illuminates and cherishes life –
Part of a line of women who walk together.

Chapter Five

PMC Weekend

S train out all the clichés people may offer up: it's lightning in a bottle, brewing some of humanity's sweetest lemonade, making sunshine out of rain.

Yet when you experience the PMC, there's still something succulent about this camp goulash.

PMCers prepare to take off at dawn from Sturbridge in 2011.

On a Wednesday before PMC weekend, its warehouse and cinder-block walled office are in full swing. Guys on two forklifts and others with pallet lifts move boxes of frozen egg patties, hot dogs, and other foodstuff out of trailers. They set them down briefly, sort and account for each load, and load the pallets back into refrigeration, ready for an assigned destination. There's a lightness of expectation in the good buzz swirling around. This is not a full-time job for most here. The core group are 20-somethings who've come back to volunteer again or are paid interns. Some Stop & Shop truck drivers are about, old hands at this mini-distribution center. The crew is vigilant, fully aware they must make a quick flip to keep the food cold, but there's nothing frenetic even with the massive kick-off only 56 hours away. Nearly everyone has the calm look of picking up where they left off last summer, as if running on some internal clock. A radio station recycling worn classic rock is duly ignored.

Rolling into his senior year of college, Alex Keefe inherited the role of Provincetown logistics coordinator from his dad. For nine years he's helped with setup and breaking down the finish line, which involves trucking about 5,000 bicycles back to their starting points. "As my father says, 'We do it because we can,'" Keefe says. His family lost three relatives, his grand-mother and two uncles, while a grandfather survived cancer. He wants to become a cop and volunteers as a call firefighter in a nearby town. There, he enlisted others to help out during one of the Kids Rides events, part of the PMC's strategy to sustain the juggernaut while offering families a good time. "We both say we hope to not do the event someday because then we've found the cure," he says.

Alex is a good friend of Matt Chase, who at age 25 coordinates ware-house logistics before and after the weekend. This is no small feat. But Chase has been involved and seen the gamut since he was six.

When trucks were unloaded by hand fire-brigade style, they sent young Matt up into a trailer to see what was there. Once he got wedged between a pallet of bike racks. "I was lodged in with my arms above my head. They had to come in and pull me out," he recalls. "It was fun." He graduated from being a runner, helped out with merchandise, and joined the road crew. Through high school and college, he and friends went site to site as jacks-of-all-trades, breaking things down and setting up for day two, and then breaking it down again. For years he caught maybe a handful hours of sleep from Friday to Sunday night. And all of the sweat equity is worth it. "You're talking about an event that touches thousands of thousands of people," he says.

His sister Amanda finishes making signs among her other duties this morning, and Matt's got three or four lists lying on her stack. Picking one up, he crosses off items with a yellow sharpie as each one gets assigned or loaded. Fruit salad in tubs. A pallet of 5,200 franks. Six thousand hamburgers and 1,400 pounds of chicken bound for Massachusetts Maritime Academy. Cookie dough, frozen brownies and pizza. Suppliers include many of the region's stalwarts: Hood, Legal Sea Foods, and Harpoon, which will provide 130 kegs. Through their constant prodding and personal connections, over the years Billy and provisions director Glynn Hawley and others have built a bulwark of in-kind sponsors. There's Sysco and Whole Foods Market, Dunkin' Donuts and some regional bakeries. Chase and his gang now move amongst the spoils.

Matt, whose real job is selling data quality software, wears black gym shorts and old running shoes. He barely breaks a sweat, briskly calling out assignments, and training his gaze now and then on a certain pallet. The week before he and Amanda had worked late with others preparing registration packets. Then some trailers left filled with signage and bike racks, plates, utensils, other dry goods and fruit. But most of the fleet—32 trucks in total, box trucks and a 56-foot-long tractor-trailer—is still here, and it's crunch time. Matt's used to things going wrong. One year a truck's brakes failed en route to the Wellesley start, so they unloaded it back-to-back to another trailer in the middle of an intersection. "You just know with this many moving parts something's going to happen," he says. "But we know we'll get it done."

Amanda Chase has ridden almost every year since turning 15, when teenagers become eligible for the full route. She actually abhors biking. "I think it's so boring, I'd rather run," she says, so after the weekend her bike usually sits in the garage until training begins the next summer. But she always relishes what she feels along the course, and observing how friends who volunteer for the first time really get it. "That's one of my favorite things to see," she says. "When you explain it to a friend they sort of know what it is, but until they're there, they don't really know." One year, she also found inspiration to write her college essay literally by a sign she spotted on a hill. Her essay worked well enough for acceptance at St. Lawrence University, where she majored in psychology and did a sports study minor. The sign read: "To the world you may be just one person, but to one person you just may be the world."

The coordination involved providing for the health and comfort and housing many of the 5,000-plus riders is a formidable feat. Some of the 200 or so corporate sponsors, who cover everything from salmon burgers to water stops, clearly use the PMC for their own marketing. It's a place where you want to be seen. This is fine with Glynn Hawley, for one. He notes that key sponsor Price Waterhouse Coopers also brings in about 75 riders and as many employees to help out, too. There are also plenty of mom and pop business connections. When Hawley sought a pizza supplier for the maritime academy, a rider told him, "I can take care of that."

A retired truck driver named Dave Aronson watches all this bustle from a corner of the warehouse. He's got a hawk-eyed look and offers more perspective. Aronson coordinates food pickups and transports gear like returning bicycles to the three starting points. To him, it's all about community. He jumped in 15 years before at the request of another driver who'd also been riding. "We come from so many different directions and we leave that here. We leave our egos at the door," he says. "This is fascinating." He smirks disclosing that he's got one of the plum jobs: "I drive the beer truck."

Inside his office Billy is engaged with someone on his Bluetooth. His grey road bike is parked alongside the wall as usual. A black t-shirt reads: "Commit. You'll figure it out." When I ask him about the theme for this year's opening ceremony speech, he points to his shirt.

"Commitment," he says. "That's what this weekend is all about."

Dave Grossman is really too sick to ride. He's got pleurisy, and the inflammation around his lungs makes breathing painful. His doctor had advised him to scratch the PMC. While she wouldn't sign off on his decision to go for it, she understood. After what seemed like a million emails to the Huckleberries about Hannah and then planning the route, Dave resisted telling the team much about his condition. All he can think about is Hannah and what she has endured.

Ushering in PMC weekend early on a Thursday morning, Dave's at a Dunkin' Donuts in Ballston Spa, greeting his Hucks as they file in. Some arrive with family members. Two friends will drive the "sag wagon," which is cycle-speak for a support vehicle carrying supplies and food. Dave considers these guys to be their guardian angels. He's about to kick off his 30th consecutive PMC and cannot anticipate all that's coming. He recently restored his first bike, a 1961 Schwinn Flying Star, to mark the anniversary. When he finishes the weekend, Grossman's daughter and wife Penny will present him with a cake. But that's a ways ahead.

A hugfest breaks out as the team reaches the Hughes's house near the town center. Hannah's and Fiona's new play set resides near a large hemlock tree and a group of neighbors and friends are on the lawn with the family. The sisters present the Hucks with purple bandanas that have "Love Hannah" written on each one. Hannah and Dave have collaborated on a team t-shirt with her drawing of a mobile huckleberry. It's set beside a picture of her in a sundress and cap which Grossman took when they met for the second time in July. Everyone puts on the shirt, each rider but Dave meeting the family for the first time.

Many of the Hucks already know something about Hannah's form of leukemia, and the mutation that causes the trouble. Joel Bard, a scientist whose work projects often involve oncology, gets to chat a little with Jeff about Gleevec®. Hughes is very excited about the drug's prospects. To her dad, so far, "the results look great," Bard reports. Yet, he also feels Jeff's reserve. Hannah is still at a delicate, if not relatively perilous, juncture. Because her immune system is so weak, the Hucks cannot actually embrace her. But they make up for that with the adults.

Hannah's parents and other relatives are blown away by the riders. "They made that little girl feel so special and so incredible and so important," Rana says later. "There was no way to convey to them how much that meant to us, that people who don't even know you believe in something so strongly." For Sandy and Garry, the stomach punch they felt when their granddaughter was diagnosed had lessened, like their own nights crying together. Sandy had suffered a fall in Boston during Hannah's recovery, breaking a knee and leg. Leaning on a cane as the cyclists came up to her, Sandy recalled, "They kept saying to us, 'Thank you, thank you,' and tears were in my face, saying, 'No, thank *you*.'"

"We didn't really know them then," she continued. "They each have a story, and they [looked] at Hannah like she [was] the best thing since sliced bread. It was pure love. It was wild. It really was."

Grossman had already given Hannah a Huckleberry Hound bobble head doll, and he had another one with him for Fiona. He handed the team's biography book to Hannah, joking that she should memorize it. She shuffled off to a chair and began pouring through it. There was also a purple Vermont Teddy Bear, and for Rana and Jeff, the cap and gown to be presented later. All in all, "It was cool," Hannah exclaims six months later on a day when Dave and I meet her at Dana-Farber.

Pushing off from Hannah's driveway, the Hucks have 84 miles to go on this first day. Each one worth it. Almost.

They quickly ride through town into fields and rolling hills, heading east first and then south, which steers them clear of Albany. Crossing the Hudson they spot a bald eagle swooping in for a meal, and the team begins serious climbing. Several members have GPS computers on their bikes, which help but don't distinguish between asphalt, gravel or dirt roads. There are some anxious moments. Tucking downhill at 40 miles per hour it suddenly turns to pot-holed dirt.

Dave's got his own Huckleberry bobble head mounted, and its head flies off the attached spring. He gets out of the mainstream of bikers and skids a while. Then he walks back uphill. He finds it. As Ellen Kirk, too, hits dirt, she is thinking, "Great, I better not do anything else." She sees Grossman panicking, but they operate successfully to revive the hound.

"It could've been worse but I guess my head was more securely fastened," Grossman notes. The team crosses the state line, enjoy supper together, and spend the night in West Stockbridge.

The next morning, the Hucks don their official team shirts. No slouch fits, these are race-cut jerseys with high collars and raglan sleeves. The cartoon hound sits astride an antique, high-wheel bike on the front, and their route is plotted on a map with sponsors' logos on the back—and a muffin. They head east, joined by a couple of other riders, making a tough climb up the Jacob's Ladder byway in the Berkshires, with a long, fast-paced downhill from there. One rider has mechanical troubles so they stop at a bike shop. Dave leads a small group off the path briefly to visit the old Huckleberry bakery in Huntington, which had closed maybe a year before.

To Kirk, at least, the detour is comical. She came aboard in 2005, occasionally flying in from as far as Tokyo for the PMC. She thought the bakery's food was horrible. And there's another cafe nearby, where no one suspects lard in the muffin batter. "I just thought, we're idiots," she says. "We could've continued going to the bad bakery and missed this, because we didn't open our eyes?"

There's another off-road stop the Huckleberries will need to make the next day. It's become a moment of unity and, perhaps, solace. Another rider lost both his mom and his wife to cancer, and the cemetery where both are interred is close to the route. "He asked a few years ago, do you mind if we stop by?" Grossman says. "Everyone takes a moment to express who they're riding for and why—it's a tearfest. After meeting Hannah and her family this year, we kind of looked at one another and said, for all the people we're riding for this year, we're riding for such a positive reason, because she's going to make it."

This stop is one of the reasons Kirk keeps coming back. At 54, the corporate strategy consultant finds herself training harder than ever. "To be a better rider, as opposed to just surviving," she says. "Wild horses couldn't keep me away." Early in the summer of 2012, a close friend of hers checked into the hospital with stomach pains. Seven days later he died of Stage 4 colon cancer. "How can that happen?" she asks. "I saw him a month

*Dave Grossman celebrated his 30th PMC ride adding
two days for Hannah Hughes in 2011.*

before, he wasn't even 60. Why do I do the PMC? I don't want that to keep happening." Ellen is also a melanoma survivor herself.

Stories roll out by those graves along the PMC route. Some speakers grow a little more composed year to year. There is laughter, and everyone reminds each other of their own humanity. Kirk says that despite the big buildup, the obsessive training and perks, the money demands and self-satisfaction, "strip all of that away. We're all there for the cause. It is the one charitable organization or charitable event that I have seen where nothing is more important than the cause. It's not about us. It's not about us."

Dave Grossman can't help but wonder how the Hughes family has done it. He doesn't know if he could. "Every parent has challenges raising their children," he writes his donors a few weeks later, "but to be put through this test with one child and then have your younger child be the life [that is] so instrumental in the recovery of her older sister...Fiona is a hero in every sense of the word."

As PMC weekend kicks off Friday afternoon in Sturbridge, Matt DeLuca is in a tent big enough to house a small circus. In another setting he might be considered an unlikely rider. Not here, where the Sturbridge Host Hotel has morphed into a bustling PMC hub once again.

It's been just six weeks since DeLuca finished chemotherapy for Hodgkin's Disease. Matt is 62, and over three decades he's run hundreds of marathons and other road races. He's also ridden in the PMC for 20 years. He lives south of Boston, an outdoorsman who hunts deer and turkeys, keeps a camp in Maine and cleans carpets and floors for a living. He and his wife would spend a month each year camping on a remote stretch of Nauset Beach, where he fly fishes and friends come by boat replenishing ice and food and spirits and spend long weekends. He knows he's fortunate, and not just because he's one of very few people who spend a month with their toes in the sand, literally without shoes on. Each work year ends with "the prize," the great ride. And then he takes off work until Labor Day.

Only the winter before DeLuca faced an inescapable yet potentially lethal irony; it's a major chord in his story. What brought him to the PMC and Dana-Farber in the first place was a Bostonian he had once taught to snowboard. Her name is Leslie Semonian. She survived Ewing's Sarcoma as a teenager but lost her battle at age 32.

Leslie was a natural people organizer, an avid traveler, and a five-time PMC rider. She also established Leslie's Links Fund, a hub of information on the rare bone cancer and a fundraising vehicle with its own legacy that's still underway. Leslie's Links supported groundbreaking discoveries led by Dana-Farber's Dr. George Demetri, director of the Center for Sarcoma and Bone Oncology. Her riding team earmarked more than $1.1 million through 2010 to the cause. One year Leslie skipped a treatment and, against doctor's orders, biked without a fibula in one leg. While strictly friends with Matt and almost 20 years his younger, she'd talk with him a few times a year and occasionally met up on ski trips organized by mutual friends. Semonian was earning her MBA when the disease returned, and she urged DeLuca to ride.

Matt's woodsman's compass struck a new heading. He'd learned to push through tremendous pain as a marathoner and on horrendous bike routes when he had hydrated way too little, and his quads locked up: it became euphoric, like passing into another dimension, and he just kept moving. Yet DeLuca had much more to experience. It was the first time he'd given to charity. He hit up a contractor pal a few days before his first PMC to get over the fundraising hump, and Matt has earmarked what he raises for Ewing's Sarcoma research ever since. "As little as I knew her, she really changed my life," he says.

His ride became a truly personal affair after his diagnosis in 2010. A lump appeared on the side of DeLuca's neck, and he figured he got it at the gym. His doctors, however, said it was Stage IV Hodgkins and one of the rarest forms. "It blew my mind," he says. "I'm one of those people who watches everything I eat, all organics." He shops at local certified farms, buys organic breads, abhors processed food and high fructose corn syrup; detergent and chemical-free, he and his wife even mix their own bug spray using essential oils, which they say kick butt. The first thing he did after hearing the news was wolf down an Italian sub for the extra nitrates. DeLuca hooked up with a world-renowned oncologist and thought he was fine with it. Until he saw other patients waiting for chemo one day, and he broke down. "I said, 'I'm no different than all those people.' My doctor waived it away. He said, 'Your life will be a mess for six months.'"

After his first six-hour treatment that winter, "just to be an idiot I went down and did 20 push-ups in front of the nurses." DeLuca had the feeling it would all be temporary, but before he got on a bike again in April, his recovery was dodgy. He'd suffered bronchitis for a month, then had influenza and could barely get up one stair. He needed to begin training. Thinking he might last 5 or 6 miles, he rode for 20, wiping himself out for five days. With only a handful of treatments left, Matt waited a bit and after the second to last ride, he did 40 miles with his friends. They braced to watch his back at the PMC. "What a gutsy move to even try it," says one of his buddies, Mickey Ahearn, who introduces us inside the tent.

Some 3,000 riders will take off at dawn tomorrow from Sturbridge, fully awake on a course with 45 initial hilly, challenging miles. A shorter, flatter ride also begins 90 minutes or so later the next morning from Wellesley, which is also the hub for one-day optional routes on Sunday. Both of the Saturday routes end at the maritime academy in Bourne.

DeLuca and a few friends gather outside the hotel, feeding on burgers, chicken, corn on the cob, salads, and chowder. Matt nurses a beer as he tells me his story. The big tent, pitched to the very edge of a pond, roars with others who meet up and begin their weekend-long feeding and carb-loading. Inside the hotel, registration cranks out as riders and their companions snatch up this year's t-shirts, sweats, and last-minute rain gear.

Matt Chase has been on his feet all day. He did get six hours of sleep Thursday night—more than his average, which isn't bad. Now he's helping at the merchandise checkout and reports that logistics are going well. So far, no trucks have gotten lost. The few calls he's gotten about missing goods were usually followed minutes later with another saying, "We found it, we checked again." Matt's parents mix nearby among the tables, reuniting with friends and firming things up. A friend of Jon's and Cindy's mentions that her daughter, who began riding with Amanda at age 15, wants to become a doctor working with cancer patients.

Around 6 p.m., Lance Armstrong enters an auditorium with Senator John Kerry through a side door for the opening ceremony. It's his first PMC appearance and this is huge, despite the pending doping scandal and Armstrong's ethical implosion. Ten years earlier, Lance had pledged to ride, and he's finally arrived.

Armstrong's legacy with his seven Tour de France wins is in question, but he hasn't plunged yet into full disgrace. Accusations loom that he, like many other cyclists, took performance-enhancing drugs. Perhaps worse, Armstrong is also alleged to have conspired to deceive the many supporters who contributed to his charity, while seeking to destroy the reputations of riders and others who spoke out against him. The debate is already under way as to whether the ends justify his means. An ethicist at *The New York Times* will point out later that the two actions are interconnected, perhaps in the same way a true tragic hero's hubris brings about his downfall. If Armstrong does not cheat, "Livestrong's ability to help people would be muted," the writer suggests, referring to his huge cancer-fighting foundation. Lance is already playing defense this summer. Just weeks before the PMC, his legal team had fired back about leaks to the media regarding a federal grand jury inquiry, saying those amounted to character assassination.

Mature and well informed, most PMCers already know that Armstrong is tarnished, if not guilty. If the hammer had already fallen from the International Cycling Union, the sport's governing body that will formally strip Armstrong of his titles 14 months later, Lance wouldn't have been welcomed near this stage.

In the months ahead, other details will emerge of lucrative business deals Armstrong cut for himself, and criticism that his foundation spent lavishly on fundraising activities and bureaucracy, failing to meet the philanthropic bar that's actually set by the PMC. In private, Starr will speak scathingly of the yellow-braceleted icon. Yet Billy will refuse to pile on in public. "There is a moral consequence," he says. "What you do matters."

Although contorted details of the doping scandal are unfolding, they are put aside for Armstrong's PMC appearance in 2011. This is Mr. Livestrong, the worldwide face, as Billy puts it, of every Living Proof rider and other cancer survivor. About 270 of them will ride the next day. Lance receives thunderous applause and the first of two standing ovations. People come up to him at his seat with shirts and posters to sign. He's in jeans and a gray windbreaker, taking a quick break from a family vacation. His agent didn't tell Billy until an hour beforehand that Lance had no speech. So Starr, reprising his brief stint as a reporter, went to his hotel room to write five or six queries for a question-and-answer session on stage.

Billy's casual in those signature khaki shorts and sandals, wearing that same emblematic black t-shirt. But casual only so much.

He admonishes everyone to settle down, reminding them, we'll do the ceremony PMC-style: on time, the right way. There's going to be a live broadcast on the popular "Chronicle" show by the PMC's new media partner, Boston's WCVB-TV, following the first hour of the opening presentation. The show's chiseled host, Anthony Everett, stands just off stage practicing to himself and gesturing his lines with a notebook open. He runs his hand through his coiffed mane. Then Starr welcomes everyone and tosses out highlights like t-shirts pumped into the crowd during a Celtics timeout. The event raised 350 percent more the previous year than all other single-event athletic fundraisers combined. Riders' average contributions were tops in the industry. After a soft year with the 2009 downturn, PMCers bounced back by 8.6 percent, way above the norm. Some 36 states are now represented, and Billy croons, this includes plenty of riders "from the great state of New Yawk." In their 13th year Kids Rides have raised more than $4 million. Ridership is now one-third female and three-quarters alumni, with average years of participation at 4.5. This weekend there are 148 riders over 65 years old. "I don't see a peak in site," he perks.

Starr mentions a college professor who wrote a paper about the PMC and other nonprofit icons, including Newman's Own, and Girl Scout cookies. He's grinning and self-aware: "I was stunned by his choice of words—me, who has pitched the PMC in so many different ways." The paper concludes, "There are no product or market substitutes for the PMC. The PMC is a singular product that donors or customers cannot buy anywhere else, on any market, at any price. If if you want the PMC experience, you have to buy into the PMC event."

When Lance comes up it's clear he doesn't yet know the event that well, but by mid-morning Saturday he will. He sent one of his yellow jerseys 12 years ago and pledged to ride. He looks out as if feigning surprise, saying, "This is a movement, this is amazing."

Channeling what might be the stump remarks he often gives at fund-raisers, Armstrong compares the whole gig to a peloton, a group of riders who stick together. Lance urges everyone to keep in mind that they're going to be needed back again. He references his foundation, which has given $3 million to Dana-Farber for survivorship care, and its support for other marquee cancer centers. Armstrong urges the centers to collaborate more and not be silos in their research or with survivorship care. Starr's questions have a light touch. Yet he's persistent as usual, aiming to glean the most possible from his famous guest. Billy asks Armstrong what it means to him that he's riding as a survivor in the PMC. Lance doesn't respond directly, but says, "I went out for a ride this morning with friends and family. I love that. It's been 15 years since I was diagnosed. I certainly didn't think we'd still be dealing with this disease."

The audience explodes. For tonight, at least, Lance is one of us. It's about the cause. He may be a liar, and most of us hate cheats, but those

Starr greets Lance Armstrong at PMC Opening
Night in 2011, more than a year before the
cycling icon's fall.

sentiments get trumped here and now. It's the cause, stupid. What this Texas renegade has done to embolden the fight.

Billy has a last one coming. It's more of a good-natured barb than a finishing question, and he's about to wear a shit-eating grin.

"Maybe next year if you train more you'll be able to ride with us for the full two days," he says, extending a hand, his face flush again.

Lance deadpans, "I don't do well with challenges."

Just before Armstrong glides in with John Kerry, his riding partner, at a water stop in Lakeville the next morning, Declan Rourke arrives with his mom and dad. Just six, Declan was able to ride his purple bike with training wheels the night before in Sturbridge. Despite Lance's appearance, this boy is actually the really big cheese this weekend.

Declan is a survivor of one of the rarest childhood cancers, Atypical Teratoid/Rhabdoid Tumor, which strikes the central nervous system. Until recently there was little hope against the tumor. After Declan had a seizure in his crib Tym and Mel Rourke instantly faced a new identity. His parents could count the survivors of AT-RT on one hand. But their son made it through 60 weeks of treatments, and even when he went from 26 to 19 pounds, never lost his winning smile. At least one biking team lends a big hand, sending contributions to DFCI researchers who developed a multi-pronged therapy regimen in 2009 that extended the life for AT-RT patients. Those treatments have even cured a few children with the disease, apparently including Declan. This year members of two teams are sponsoring him, Team Kermit, and the Stem Cell Cyclists.

Declan and his parents are introduced at the opening night ceremony, where he wheels buoyantly across the auditorium floor. Tym takes to the microphone, thanking riders and conveying his belief in the power of stories. He thanks Dana-Farber, implying that it alone had the guts to devote resources to a disease that only 32 kids in the country had at the time. Rourke recalls how he'd never felt more in his skin than on February 24, 2005, the day Declan was born. Then he leaves everyone breathless.

"He is alive because of you," Rourke says, his soft voice beginning to rise, sharpening. "He gets a first base hit because of you. He gets to graduate kindergarten—a boy who was not expected to live through pre-school—because of you." Not unexpectedly, when Declan got his first bike, immediately he wanted to help the cause. In his first year, he was the top fundraiser in a Kids Ride in Concord, New Hampshire.

Rourke asks everyone to do two things over the weekend. Stop at the Pedal Partners tent and meet the kids and some teams. Second, listen. "Listen to everything around you: the sun on your face, the burn in your

Dozens of children's faces greet riders at the Pedal Partners' stop.

legs as you climb up that hill, the cheers as you go down that hill...two simple words: 'Thank you,' 'Thank you,' 'Thank you,' 'Thank you.'"

If riders needed any further motivation, it is reinforced in Lakeville, a small town near the southeast coast. Riders have come as far as 83 miles. Soon it will break 80 degrees, with the humidity rising, and they've got maybe 25 more to go to complete the first day.

Alongside a knoll rising up to the high school, Jen Tolo is among those cheering beside a succession of dozens of posters, each with a child's face and name. Her son Brodie is one of them, as is Hannah. He also has ALL, and like Hannah, Brodie has a great chance of remaining free from recurrence for at least five years. He celebrated his sixth birthday a day before the PMC, and he is one of 73 children paired with a team. His mom had ridden for Brodie the previous three years.

"I'm glad I know what that's like," Tolo says. "I'm glad to know. My family was standing right here cheering last year, my son had a sign that read, 'I'm five and I'm alive.'" She knows what good energy is, Living Proof riders, cyclists wearing buttons and portraits of remembrance. Someone

Kids join the Lego table at the Pedal Partners' tent in 2012.

who asked her, "How's it going, mom?" Waves of inspiration, perhaps once bottled up, now unkempt and free. "That's what got me up those hills, knowing he had to suck it up," she says as Brodie plays nearby. "Everyone has a tie to cancer. This is about the passion that's here now."

Up by the Pedal Partners' tent, riders drop their bikes and head towards the kids. Many of the adults are meeting the children for the first time.

The Huckleberries come in. They pause, entering the parking lot, to don their new t-shirts and purple bandanas. Hannah's family is all here, joined by Sandy and Garry, plus three friends. They had followed the team across the state Saturday in the RV, Grossman texting Rana with updates.

Even here, Rana cannot fully gauge how this will impact each of them. Hannah's in a sun tent when the team pulls up, and soon they're playing with a beach ball and conversing with stuffed animals beside her and Fiona. Pictures are snapped and a few spouses join in. "You couldn't have met nicer, more open people," Rana says. "One's mom is a three-time cancer survivor. All they had been through, and still they wanted to reach out."

Grossman tells Hannah, "if my numbers are right, when you turn 13, I think we're going to have a big party, and I think I'm going to start taking a collection for a purple bike." He suggests she might consider riding when she turns 15. But Hannah stands her ground. "With strings attached," she counters, which ushers in a running joke between them, since riding isn't among her favorite things.

The team gives high fives as they ride away, and Dave is last to leave. He doesn't hold anything back. It's in his face, ruddy, trim, and open, that's who he is, and this again touches Rana and Jeff. "It was way beyond what we thought it was going to be," she says. And she journals the next day, "It is a gift that goes far beyond anything I could have anticipated. To watch Hannah greet the team and know these people are supporting her, rooting for her, and care about her because they are that committed to making a difference reminds me that the donation of a person's time has such a great impact... They raised an eight-year-old girl's spirit, fed her with positive energy, and made her smile more in one day then I had seen in quite a while."

"It just kind of rekindles the human spirit," she offers a few months later. "What we're supposed to be like. I know it sounds sort of cheesy, but we've become so jaded. I hope my eight-year-old and five-year old can hold on to that."

Behind the Hugheses, kids under the tent are making collages and waving bubble wands. Declan Rourke and his parents are here, expecting to meet Declan's riding teams. Samantha Mattos, a college student who is studying theatre, wears a Sherlock Holmes detective cap. She can't

The Hucks greet Fiona, Hannah, and family members in 2011.

wait to do more face painting with the kids, and she's got some demos on her legs to show them. "It's going to be a zoo" soon, she says. Outside, other children sit in beach chairs or play volleyball.

Armstrong and Senator Kerry spend about 15 minutes beside the Pedal Partners' enclave. Scott Brown, Massachusetts' other senator, is also a rider, but he is not with them now. Lance signs autographs and Kerry, a nine-year rider and survivor who is among the top "Heavy Hitters" donors, downs a banana (he will contribute more than $220,000 this year, while Senator Brown raises more than $39,000). Kerry rests a few minutes on a golf cart beside the throng before joining Armstrong again for photos. Young kids flock to Lance, who doesn't seem to mind. When Dana McCreesh approaches with her son Brent, who is another Pedal Partner, she begins to tell Lance how Brent is a triathlete. He asks her to spread out the shirt he's signing. At some point, Armstrong promises to ride again. They mount and the buzz moves on, with a Kerry sag SUV in tow.

The Pedal Partners program is a mixed blessing that requires a gentle touch. That spring there were 77 teens and kids involved, but several had died before the PMC weekend. Others were not well enough to come out, as Hannah could not for an event at Fenway Park held that May. "We're never really pushing for a high number," says coordinator Alex Smith.

She has the difficult task of managing the relationships after meeting families at the hospital, where Smith is often doing arts and crafts with children and covered in glitter, which helps ease the introductions. It's a complicated balancing act. Some team members, if they're a little too self-absorbed, hold high expectations for their involvement with families, whereas parents like Jeff and Rana Hughes have a singular focus. Smith tries to match them up geographically. Most often the mutual benefits extend far. Particularly for children early in treatment, she observes, "parents might feel hopeless and isolated, and it helps turn them around. It gives the kids something to look forward to."

Two water stops ahead, a freshening breeze is coming off Buzzards Bay as the riders reach the Massachusetts Maritime Academy. For many, this brings relief and more reunion and some downtime before the second day.

PMCers have again taken over the campus on the west end of the Cape Cod Canal, a series of brick-faced and modern buildings and cadet dorms fanning out on a small peninsula. Tents are wedged everywhere beside academic halls and on the grass of the playing fields, and teams meet up for photo shoots beside the canal. All afternoon riders hit the chow lines and stretch out in small groups. BMW, the sponsor of this hub site, showcases its new models on the baseball outfield beside a posh, air-conditioned cool-down tent. There's live music on stage, a rock band, followed by an R&B quartet from Boston.

Only a few participants appear to be openly nursing significant pains. One man stretches on an exercise ball and several riders ice down their muscles. Others relax by their tents or walk the gangplank to a training ship, the T.S. Kennedy, to check out their accommodations. A 90-foot yacht tied up at the dock hosts one team whose leader works for Goldman Sachs. Libations flow under a separate tent, and one server jokes that anyone seeking his first Harpoon may now skip to the front.

Mike Kelleher, Jr., a seven-year rider, and his dad Michael, twice that as a volunteer, meet up near the dock. Both seem to be thriving in this fiesta of second winds. Senior wears a floppy straw hat with Hawaiian leis hanging on his chest. His son mentions coming across three generations riding together this day, topped off by an 81-year-old man.

"My thing is, 70 percent of people here are athletic, able-bodied, but 30 percent haven't ridden since their BMX as a kid," Mike says. "You see them, and they need to be here, there's someone, there's a physical output of this emotion. That's very impactful for me, seeing people's emotions. That's part of the attraction, being a part of something bigger than yourself."

His dad used to ride with a group called the North Shore Cyclopaths that included Starr's cherished mentor, Sam Zoll. Kelleher, too, has plenty to reminisce about regarding his late friend the judge. Zoll had died of advanced gall bladder cancer that spring at age 76. A native son of Salem, Zoll began a paper route at age eight and helped feed his family with the proceeds during the Depression, continuing the job for 15 years. During a short stint as the city's mayor he helped redevelop its waterfront, and for years he regularly swam off an an island in the harbor. Sam was recognized wherever he went, says Kelleher, who unwinds a yarn or two that reveals Zoll's relish for fabricating tall tales.

His death hit Starr hard. As Billy told a gathering of top donors in May just a few weeks after Zoll had passed, Sam pointed an ethical compass by which Starr could measure his own heading. He set the bar for what public service means. For many years, Sam regarded himself as the PMC's consultant without a portfolio. "Just good counsel," Billy reflected in front of 500 donors and sponsors inside Boston's gleaming InterContinental Hotel. That evening, there had been plenty to crow about again. The PMC's lead gift to Dana-Farber helped the institute complete a $1.2 billion capital campaign, and a ribbon-cutting for a new plaza honoring the Pass-Mass was set for the next month. Big donors had raised 60 percent of last year's PMC total, while registration and volunteers were also up. All huge things. Yet Starr got choked up noting the loss of both Zoll and another longtime rider, Gordon Young. He doesn't forget those who brought him and the PMC to such heights.

Back beside the canal, I meet someone who has her own connection to another lasting legacy. Nancy Shepard sits refreshed after enjoying a

Sam Zoll in his office. Courtesy of Salem News.

15-minute massage, which she calls her best work over in years. She has ridden in from Wellesley and is an old friend of one of Billy's early and closest riding mates, Todd Miller, who is PMC royalty. Shepard wasn't always a PMCer and didn't even own a bike when Miller died. Yet she and many of Todd's other friends continue to carry forward his passion to give back and take it to the outer limit. His story is another vital arc in this circuitry.

There wasn't much that Todd Miller didn't do that he set out to accomplish. He survived Hodgkin's Disease twice as a teenager, diagnosed initially when he was 14. "Do it now" became his motto and amplitude. The lanky, often bearded, Long Island native was a math whiz who worked for a while at Fidelity in mutual funds accounting. He also developed an unforeseen knack teaching people the nuances of road biking. His widow Valerie relishes the days when Todd worked in an emporium making 5-gallon batches of amazing stuff like chocolate peanut butter and cantaloupe ice cream. He didn't bother making long-term plans as he pursued oversized goals. He lived another 23 years cancer-free until his early 40s when a secondary disease emerged in his lungs, and he could not beat it back.

Already an avid cyclist, Miller met Starr the fall after the first ride, apologizing that he'd missed it. By next summer he was hooked. Todd pledged to ride as long as he lived; he made good on that for 17 of his next 18 years. He'd do anything Billy asked. An eager PMC spokesman in TV public service spots, for videos shown at the pre-event dinners, or speaking at orientations and traveling the state. He also raised nearly a quarter million dollars as one of the event's top fundraisers during that span. One year, expecting once again to beat his personal record in pledges, Miller told a reporter, "This is my way of saying thank you." He, too, embraced the big party, like another Deadhead bumping into someone you haven't seen for years on the concert floor. Offering a quick, glowing greeting—and off he shuffles again.

Todd and Billy were weekend cycling soulmates. "A sweet, good person," Starr says. "You share certain viewpoints or passions, humor, families. You spend time, it was easy. We were of a similar mind." With his collection of old maps Todd knew all the backroads and over 10 years helped Starr develop the classic Sturbridge-Provincetown route. Like Billy, he got ticked when early riders had to walk their bikes over the Sagamore Bridge.

For several years they did "the solstice ride" together—Val dubs it "the long ridiculous ride"—leaving western Massachusetts before dawn and crossing to the outer Cape, some 300 miles, by the evening. They chatted NBA finals, those Bird-Magic-DJ-Worthy epics of the mid-80s, to new routes to sweet spots, and revamped their dreams along the way. To spice things up before the PMC's 111-mile first leg, Todd sometimes came down from Vermont with the renown "Magic Mountain" crew, whose idea of upping the challenge a tad might be a five-day trek from Canada. The best ride in the northeast, Bobbi Miller recalls her son reporting, was up Cadillac Mountain on Mount Desert Island. One year he did more than 7,000 miles including 20 century rides (more than 100 miles in a day). Val supported all this "because they were Todd's way of celebrating his health," Billy recalls. She, too, rode sometimes, starting about 1984 when riders bunked at Camp Bournedale—"bunks in the fog, disgusting, you go to sleep damp and wake up damp, but the nice part is you wake up in the forest," Val says. "You'd do the first part together and ride along the canal, and then he'd be gone. I trained to dance on the boat coming home, never mind the ride."

To his friends, Todd never seemed more at home than when on his bike. "He was unflappable," says Ted Merritt, who first joined Miller for the PMC in 1986. "The feeling he exuded to me, everything was kind of smooth." Along the route, Miller would deftly signal to his mates, shaking a water bottle as a reminder to drink, or pointing down to show a hazard on the road.

Miller and Starr had a mid-summer tradition, taking a ride on the last Wednesday night before the PMC. Todd would help his friend tamp down his nerves. "He just helped me calm down. We did what we did best—ride, and we talked," Starr says. A decade later Todd was diagnosed with lung cancer, which claimed his life in 1998. Despite his treatments, Miller still managed to ride parts of both days the year before.

"He was a fighter," his mother says. "He was obsessed in a healthy productive way because in his mind if he could ride, the cancer was gone. And it drove him, because he wanted to live. He figured every day was a gift and when he rode his bike, it seemed to me he was keeping himself healthy in his mind. That's why he probably lived longer than other people who don't do these things. He had a drive."

Bill Hahn was Miller's doctor. He's among at least 100 physicians, nurse practitioners and other DFCI staffers who ride, plus untold others from lab technicians to facilitators who do the PMC or its sister event, the Jimmy Fund Walk. He and Todd formed their own team off the bicycles as provider and patient. Miller's resilience, in some form, was never vanquished. "He had been through a lot," Hahn begins. "He was never down at all; he was always 'Let's figure out what it is and figure out how to take care of this.' He didn't want sugarcoating, he wanted to know what was going on."

"He would do whatever in his power he could to not have it affect what he was doing. His philosophy was very much you make something of every day," Hahn says. "To me that was very inspiring. As an oncologist, you want to do the best for every patient; you can't help each one. Some patients you really feel like you help the person and family get through something, but in some, it's a partnership. He helps you as much as you do him."

Miller is memorialized on the "PMC Bridge to Progress," a skyway connecting buildings at Dana-Farber with a plaque and the rear-view mirror from his bike. Hahn passes this tribute as he heads to his office each day. To him it's so fitting since part of the ride is about remembrance. "While riding you have time to think about the people you've lost along the way, and I think it reminds you why you're doing this," Hahn says. "It doesn't matter if you're tired or hurt or facing a 20-mile-an-hour headwind. You know that doesn't matter at all."

Nancy Shepard continues riding, and by 2011, after 12 years of riding, she'd raised about $155,000 for the cause. Once she did part of the course only months after breaking her pelvis, another time while suffering a stomach ulcer. She's no heroine, but cringes when she hears people complain about their jobs or relatively minor health issues.

"Whenever I see a bike rider on the road I think of Todd and his love of riding, his kindness of spirit and love of family," she says. "I tell Todd's mom, Todd would be laughing at what a bike queen I've become."

*Living Proof survivors gather for a toast at the
Massachusetts Maritime Academy.*

In 1998, every rider starting over the Bourne Bridge passed a large portrait of him. Beginning "Miller's mile," as the poster said, many slowed for a moment to touch Todd.

Sheets of rain awaken riders during the overnight in Bourne, and many get out of the dorm beds, bunks or their own tents by 4 a.m. on Sunday. No matter how many miles you log, it's always tough to sleep well this weekend, Dave Grossman admits to his supporters. Still, when his Hucks take off along the canal at 5:15 a.m., the rain has mostly let up. Refreshed, they begin to feel their second wind (or fourth, actually) kicking in. Near Nickerson State Park about halfway through the ride, they pass a PMC icon who is riding for the first time.

Using only his left leg, Jack O'Riordan just keeps pedaling.

Two weeks shy of his 16th birthday, by some measures O'Riordan, like Matt DeLuca, should be home on the couch. Or on the sidelines in crutches. He broke an ankle early in the summer riding at a BMX track—his second intended 360 "was a 340," his mom says. Jack's doctors told him he couldn't push off his right foot, but that wasn't enough to stop him.

When he was only a year old, after being diagnosed with a kidney cancer called Wilms Tumor, doctors found that it spread to 10 tumors on his lungs. At the time, he was one of only six children in the country with this form of the disease. That led to an intense but short regimen of radiation, and then 54 weeks of chemo. Jack was the PMC's youngest celebrity for years, a next-generation poster boy after Todd Miller. At the Brewster water stop where his family has long volunteered, they made a sign with his portrait and updated it every year. At first, the poster read, "I'm three...thanks to you!" Jack became a legend standing beside it. Riders would pause, touch Jack, and often take an emotional moment before continuing on.

Jack's changed his sign to, "I'm 15 and riding thanks to all you." His inspiration hasn't altered one bit.

For his first PMC, O'Riordan was one of six captains on the Cape Cod Sea Camps team, which is named Team Schuyler for an 18-year-old battling cancer for a second time. Jack is the only team member in remission. But after his crash, he could only really train for seven days on a stationary bike. During the ride he's outfitted with a triple-padded cast and special cushion underneath the ankle, with only his left foot clipped in. One by one, riders and bystanders press him onward like kisses of sea spray.

> *Oh my god, is that even safe? Keep going, wow! Keep going, keep going, keep going—Oh, my God!*
> *We've got a Jack sighting!*
> *Crippled but free. I was blind all the time I was learning to see.*

His first thought is: Pedal. "I thought I'd go back and say hi to everyone and I ended up riding with them most of the first day," he says. As he tires, he puts his mind to it again, saying later, "I wanted to keep on, don't stop until you hit the end." There's a brutal stretch of hills early on day one, and he catches a ride with his parents. But O'Riordan cycles about 180 miles, doing the full route the second day.

How the heck? others ask. "I have no idea either," Jack says. "The experience was just mind-blowing."

Throughout his illness and recovery, O'Riordan's family gained new perspective. "It's a weird thing, but it's been worth it," his mother Chris says. "I don't know if I had to go back in time if I would change anything. It's changed our family for the better. He values things in life more than other 16-year-olds." When things go sour, the family can usually handle it.

Rounding the corner towards the Lower Cape for the final 35 miles or so, riders relish a strong tailwind. The rain-slicked roads and slippery highway striping exact a toll. In a stretch from Brewster to Wellfleet more than 15 cyclists crash. There's also one car collision, and six riders are taken to the hospital. One suffers a broken pelvis. But these are sustainable injuries and expected. "It's going to happen," Billy predicts matter-of-factly a few months earlier when discussing the typical hazards, but not without empathy. By almost any measure the PMC's safety record has been pretty good. Cyclists do about a combined 750,000 miles on a weekend. Almost anyone who requires a hospital visit goes home the same day.

The Hucks, meanwhile, are like a well-oiled machine and have few difficulties. They pick up the pace on the Cape Cod bike path and do some crazy sprinting up climbs along the shore into Wellfleet. During some pace lining along Route 6 heading towards the finish, each Huckleberry takes a pull at the front. There's a final team photo at the finish, and everyone showers, changing into shorts and retrieving luggage. Most take their bikes over to one of the transport trucks. And they skedaddle again for another year.

Other cyclists come around Race Point. In the last five miles they fight a stiffening southerly wind, the earliest arrivals dodging more oncoming rain, their spirits lifting as a grey front pushes over the bay. Cowbells clamor again at the finish line. A small gauntlet of supporters and red-shirted volunteers roar with each approach, including Michael Kelleher wearing his crazy straw hat. Some riders arrive dazed, others giddy and slapping their mates. A few are speechless, still obstinate and fixed ahead.

As they pass through, for a handful of riders, something inside breaks open as a spitting shower resumes.

"I'm 75!" one silver-haired man exclaims with a thumbs up.

"Okay, I'm not going to do this again for a long time," a younger guy puffs.

The finishing exaltations transcend the grind of training and commuting through traffic slogs. Helmets and personalized jerseys defy life's switchbacks: yellow thunderbolts and pink flamingos; there's Team Kermit; a group sporting raccoon tails; a large and scruffy Team Bruins member with his silver Stanley Cup replica on a black iron worker's-styled helmet. Eight women in pink holler with arms aloft. Two Red Sox wives from Team 9 dismount.

A middle-aged couple comes in together, a red rose attached to both helmets, a curly-haired young woman's image on their shirts. There are no words between them, which seems apropos. Then come the Crack O'Dawn riders—"Absolved by light we decide to go on"—their logo is a halved Steal Your Face skull. Their training ethic is, Be there by 5:45 a.m. "or ride alone." Team Forza-G arrives, the "Porkapalooza" barbecue sandwich purveyors.

A group of 10, also in pink, ride for Meghan McCarthy as the "Tewksbury Tough." She is a young woman who captained her field hockey team and battled a brain tumor that claimed her life during her senior year. On the back of each rider's jersey, along with McCarthy's image is the phrase, "Have Faith Believe in Miracles." There's also Team Brew Crew; Angels on Board sporting golf balls; and seven men from Team Suzie Q. A pod of supporters break off to greet them. The clasps are tight and long and one woman wipes away tears.

Alan Starr, who is just as competitive as his cousin, finishes his extended PMC weekend. He is the same age, and like Billy remains leather-lean and sinewy, with the squint of someone who's ducked a lot of road glare. He is president of Boston Showcase Company, once their grandfather's business. Alan actually snapped the ball on Billy's failed chutzpah-call back in junior high, and for years they played tennis and squash together. He's also a terrific cyclist with two decades in the PMC, and rides with his wife and sons. While there's a hint of familial rivalry, Alan is not unsupportive of Billy's accomplishments. He's very proud of being part of the family, and the event. "There's no way to leave it without a very good strong feeling about what you're doing," he says.

This time Starr started outside Montreal, winding through Vermont over hills and beside lakes to Sturbridge over four days. He's part of a small group—it begins with 11, including a couple from Florida who are friends of his—that does this because they have each just turned 60. They complete 590 miles under mostly clear and bright skies, staying at picturesque inns along the way.

"Having a good excuse to do a little extra riding, that's kind of what it was all about," he says. Family members join him in Sturbridge and they ride the next two days together. Collectively they will raise about $25,000. Alan Starr says he would love to ride from Quebec again, if he can take the time off. "When I was done the six days of riding, I was ready to keep riding. I wasn't tired, but there wasn't any other place to ride to."

As the sky unloads in Provincetown many walk their bikes and duffel bags along Commercial Street toward the ferries and buses. Some outfit themselves in trash-bag ponchos they grabbed at the finish line party. Some pause at the Monkey Bar, one of the first alcohol stops on the way, and a crowd sprawls out the door by early afternoon. Others grimace and a few stern-eyed gents make their way against the slanting rain and fomenting P-town social scene. A handful make one last short ride to the wharf.

Dave Grossman boards a bus back to Wellesley. It's been 371 miles and 15,622 feet of climbing. Even though the bus takes an extra hour, he doesn't mind. "After 30 years of riding this event, I have pretty much outgrown the party ferry," he writes donors, "and this was one of those years I was thankful to be on the bus, even in Cape traffic." Riding four days with pleurisy, he may have done some permanent damage to his lungs, and in the months ahead his doctor will examine scar tissue. But that's not even on his screen this afternoon. When he gets back, Dave's wife Penny and daughter Hayley greet him. Ushering him into their dining room, there's a cake celebrating his 30th ride, with his old red Schwinn on top. It's almost a shame to cut it.

The main cabin of a small ferry heading to Plymouth is nearly filled with 40 or so PMCers. Their bikes are bungeed on the top deck as the boat heads into 25-knot winds and a decent chop. It's an alternate route back, and many more riders take the bigger ships to Boston. A few guys nurse beers or a gin and tonic in coffee cups. Others slump in seats still in their eye-popping PMC windbreakers.

The men poke fun at each other and then listen intently as one explains a piece of broken equipment or an accident. There is weariness and no signs of regret. John Coughlin, who is 59 and a survivor of colon cancer, rode for his seventh year and says he'll be back. He was diagnosed eight or nine years earlier, and he scoffed at the thought when they gave him little chance, Coughlin began riding after his daughter was diagnosed with cancer on her 21st birthday. She, too, persevered. Just two weeks ago she had given birth to a girl, his first grandchild.

Even a crash near the end of the first day when a rider stopped inexplicably in front of him, and never apologized, could not douse Coughlin's spirit. "This is my favorite weekend of the year," he says. "I look forward to it more than Christmas. Unfortunately then I'll have to go back to all the assholes" in the work world.

Matt DeLuca is on board, too. Before starting on Saturday, he felt a few nerves and once again realized he needed to learn something new. "In the past I'm out front pulling everyone along. This year I had to be behind everyone," he tells me. "I had some doubts the first 25 miles, but with distance, the farther I got, the better I felt." Remembering his friend Leslie Semonian provided extra motivation, as did knowing there are many people in beds who can barely move.

A few days later DeLuca sat in his office writing thank-you's to 201 donors as e-mails and calls continued to fly in. "I'm still high from the weekend," he was saying. "The high lasts a week."

Mickey Ahearn, pondering life in-between his 31 PMC weekends, chuckles, "We've all had our challenges." Career upheavals and divorce, substance abuse battles, sudden deaths and draining, anticipated loss to disease.

Mickey's another of Todd Miller's pals, and many of their old crew still ride together. He's got pieces of Todd's bike, a steel-lugged, canary yellow Serotta in his basement. Billy Starr had actually given it to Miller as a surprise gift in 1995. He convinced the manufacturer to pony up, knowing $3,000 was a lot for a bike at the time. "Nobody deserved it more," Starr says. Ahearn rode the Serotta for many years and after 20,000 miles asked for a duplicate. Every year friends carry a part from Miller's original, a piece of a spoke, or an old tire patch. They pass around his photo and follow certain other rituals. "Just carrying him with you, you know, it's pretty straightforward," Mickey says. "You want to have him around. You know he's all ready."

Jack O'Riordan, one leg in a cast, with Isabella Shaw, also a cancer survivor, in 2011. Courtesy Chris O'Riordan.

Someone still books a room at the Provincetown Inn where dozens of friends pile in for showers, champagne, and a lineup of nips, a showcase of temporary opulence, and they unwind in the pool. A couple from Minneapolis flew out once again. Another old friend rode one day and then headed over to the Vineyard. "I just connected with everyone I wanted to connect with and I'm grateful for that," Ahearn says a day later. Mickey notices the growing number of riders' kids involved—250 were age 21 or younger, signs of Billy's farm-system efficacy—and he senses things moving in the right direction.

"If you could pass some of this along to your children, giving back, I don't think you could go wrong with that," he says. "Maybe that's the take away."

Chapter Six

Her Skip Returns

Hannah took more strides forward in the months following the PMC in 2011. She came off antibiotics and had surgery to remove her central transfusion line, the double-lumen catheter. It was another huge day, which would bring more independence and eliminate a potential source of infection. Soon she'd be swimming again and taking a bath without worries. The flip side would be frequent needle sticks for her blood work.

In agreement with Hannah's doctor in Albany, Rana and Jeff allowed her to guide the decision on when to take out the line. By the end of August, Hannah's line site was healing "beautifully, her counts looking better," her mom wrote in the online journal. At times the heat took a toll so they made sure her air conditioning breaks were frequent to keep her body temperature down. On occasion she was sick at night.

The entire family entered another busy stretch as fall began. Fiona started kindergarten and Rana returned to teach third grade. She was thankful for friends, neighbors and her colleagues who supported the family during most of a year off. Their contributions had helped the Hugheses rent an apartment for those 40 days in Boston. Jeff took the lead taking his daughter to her frequent appointments, and Hannah began home tutoring three times a week, while Grandma Sandy or Garry cared for her each workday. Hannah wrote each day in a journal and watched regular episodes of the Cooking Network, making dishes using the recipes of Sandy's Italian relatives. But over this period, her grandmother found, "I could see she needed some socialization." Being primarily around adults became a crutch.

As restrictions were lifted, once-little things became big again. Mother and daughter went shopping at Target near closing time. Fiona's soccer coach asked Hannah to be the team's manager. And one day in September, she was invited to a friend's birthday party. Jeff drove her and Rana was nervous. Would she feel out of place, need to be reminded of the sun, or bugs, using hand gel, and not getting too close to the others? When she came home, "I began the interrogation. I wanted to know every detail and how Hannah felt about it all. She just stopped and looked at me and said, 'Mom, you can't even believe how much fun I had...it was so great.' And off she skipped." Rana realized she'd been worried for herself. Other firsts that she had fretted over transpired without a problem. Hannah asked about helping around the house and making her bed to earn an allowance, and they agreed.

The family wouldn't forget the outpouring from their community. Rana, half kidding, says that Ballston Spa feels like Dr. Seuss's "Whoville." A genuinely modest, small town of 5,600 people that's about 25 miles north of Albany, the average household income is $37,000. It's got its characters, and a rural heart. The winter before, Rana's friends at her school in neighboring Saratoga Springs organized a fundraiser called "Health Hope and Happiness for Hannah" hosted by two local restaurants. The room was packed and they skyped the family at the hospital. Hannah was receiving chemo at the time. "She's on the bed and leans into me and says I feel like I'm going to get sick, and Fiona fell down between a crack in the bed and was crying—with people on the other end" watching, Rana recalls. "And it was one of those moments when it was like, 'This is our life.'" Jeff remembers reading how much they would need these core supports if they were to emerge intact as a family. "And we had it," he says.

Early in 2012, the skip in Hannah's step returned in full. One day her dad watched her do a little pirouette before landing on the couch, and he felt she had just turned a big corner. Maybe six months before that they had been carrying her up to bed. And If she had had a few 10-minute bursts of energy to play, that was plenty. Their ordeal wasn't near over yet. Still to come were plenty of shots, and continuing medications, all of which she'd learned how to pronounce. But there was a long weekend with friends at Lake Placid, with all the girls out ice skating. Even Hannah, who's always had orthopedic issues like difficulty turning her feet and tight hamstrings, and for whom learning to ride a bike had been hard. On the ice she often has a large cone to push and "really only skates one one leg, and she could care less," Rana muses. "I wish I could have more of that." Hannah's blood count numbers were improving. They'd bounced around, in part due to the medications. Meanwhile, she rejoined other activities such as 4H club.

While keeping watch for every sign—her first spiking fever, or when the flu went through their house—they marveled at how she was growing up, fighting to be well with her whole being. Looking back to a few weeks before the transplant, Rana again saw how her daughter had spent hours in the hospital making valentine cards for the staff, drawing on her iPad, even putting her treatments on a calendar.

Her mom discovered that "Hannah needs to be able to express herself and weigh in on what she needs. I tend to reassure her by saying that I will take care of everything. That wasn't enough this time. She needed to be a part of how to manage her pain. I was impressed that Hannah could articulate her needs and once she did, what a difference in her outlook. This experience, for any child, makes them grow up so fast. They have to deal with things way before they should have to."

Fiona receives an equal share of the adults' marvel. Even though Rana had worried a year before that her youngest wasn't getting the attention she needed, Fiona was fine. As she grasped what being a donor meant, "she sort of took on ownership of wanting to be that helper," her mom says. Fiona inspires others outside of the family as well. Among the Huckleberries, Kirk adores her. "The bond between them is not just emotional, but physical," Ellen says. "Fiona exercised free will in a way that few people ever get the opportunity to do. She is a beautiful little pixie who doesn't have a mean bone in her body. She is the embodiment of service at the age of six or seven."

I met Hannah with her parents at Dana-Farber one day that February. Dave Grossman rode his bike from the office to see them as well. She was back mainly for immunizations and some blood work, and was soon munching on snacks and pork tenderloin before the appointment. Feisty and full of energy, she helped finish stories her mom told. One was about a sort of wardrobe malfunction during a school play, when the butterfly on her magic wand got stuck on her head.

Hannah wasn't looking forward to the shots, but seemed glad to see Dave again. He reminded her of the promised purple bike when she turns 13, "with one asterisk," they intoned together. This refers to their agreement, or the "condition" that when Hannah turns 15, she will join the Hucks on the ride. Yet cycling is not high on her top hits list. For a while she sat cross-legged on a chair, focused on the adults' conversation. "My three favorite things," she interjected at one point, "are Harry Potter, Cheez-Its, and chocolate."

Her hair had grown back to bob length, and more stories would emerge about that. One is that Hannah wanted to shave it off for a boy at her mom's school who has bone cancer. St. Baldrick's Day was approaching the next month. St. Baldricks is a nationally known charity dedicated to childhood cancer research, another major goodwill momentum-builder, and most of its fundraisers are head-shaving events at local venues like ice hockey rinks. The idea of Hannah getting a buzz cut didn't thrill her dad. However, Jeff and his father-in-law soon had their heads shaved for the cause.

That spring Grandma Sandy, who has a thing for the impromptu, took the girls to the hairdresser. Without Rana knowing, they got streaks added: pink for Fiona and orange front and back for Hannah. "It's payback for me," their mother laughed. "'Hair extensions,' she called it, but it was dyed hair. It was payback for tattoos when I was in college."

As Hannah went into the gift shop to buy something for Fiona—butterfly earrings, since her sister recently had had her ears pierced—it felt natural listening even more closely to her parents and considering all they'd gone through. People they probably never would have met had touched their lives. Rather than cloister and close themselves off, which is a natural response for many people, Jeff and Rana had opened up.

Here was Dave in spandex riding gear, gushing about their interactions last summer, beaming as he looked ahead. Both girls had lifted his team, which together raised more than $180,000 for the hospital—not earmarked for the type of ALL Hannah faces. Dave had raised $16,000 himself. A year earlier, a woman who lost her son to a rare disease reached out to Rana from an unspeakable place just before Hannah first came to Boston. She offered mom a direct line to a nurse at the clinic. "I was not ready to talk about my journey ahead," Rana wrote, "but it gave me comfort just to have her number in my wallet."

She felt things calming down a little. Her daughters entering a new phase of their own relationship, a tad older, more friendly chit-chatting. Hannah's self-confidence was building. With her doctor they discussed the timing of re-entering Hannah in school. "Now it's like starting over again," Rana said.

Chapter Seven

The Wheel Turns

W hile relishing the break after PMC weekend, many riders soon begin planning for next year, sending donors thank-you notes and restarting the wheel once again. The challenge is two-fold, both training and raising money, and there is no shortage of inventiveness for either. Some riders dispatch successive rounds of letters to supporters with research updates and their emotional appeals. Teams like the Huckleberries distribute full accounts with their photos and reflections formatted in pdf files. A group of food and wine lovers, Team Rialto-TRADE, held a cocktail party in Harvard Square joined by several top chefs and bartenders, part of their goal to raise $100,000.

Matt DeLuca, for one, makes a bold pitch. He tells donors outright that he'd like at least $75 if they can afford it, and most of his contributions range from $75 to $150. "It's a little easier for me, because I have a lot of clients and friends that I know who back me," he admits. He feels his target is doable since "a lot of them spend that to have their floors maintained" each week, which Matt does to make a living. "Or, I'll go up to a friend and say, 'Just give me $100.' What are they going to do?" In 2011, he raised close to $17,000 with about 200 sponsors. This was almost twice his average contribution, and he attributes it as sympathy for his own bout with cancer. "They threw it all away" on me, he cracks.

Shortly before his 17th PMC in 2002, Chris McKeown contacted supporters by email for the first time.

Just as with so many other participants, his list of neighbors and relatives who've struggled with disease was long, and at times, staggering. That year, McKeown was riding in honor of a family whose 10-year old daughter, Lindsay, had passed away on Memorial Day weekend from neuroblastoma. His old friend Jim Buchanan is Lindsay's dad. Chris shared this with donors:

> *Through both of their daughter Lindsay's bouts with cancer, they were able to show all of us who could really only watch, exactly what love, caring, affection, commitment and strength, means. Their lessons taught me how to address this with my daughter Maddy—in particular with the story below.*
>
> *At our dinner table on the evening of Lindsay's funeral, Lisa [McKeown's wife] asked me in "parent's speak" about the funeral. We don't shield Maddy (then five) or Griff (then three) from life's trials, but we don't purposefully expose them either. We had not gone into any detail with them about Lindsay. But kids are amazingly astute; as any parent knows. I was trying to tell Lisa about Lindsay's dad's point that there are widows and there are orphans, but no word exists for a parent who loses a child. I felt myself becoming emotional, and, as both kids were looking over their shoulders, out the window, I slipped out the back door to "check the grill." I had a brief cry, pulled myself together, and went back inside. Immediately, Maddy asked "Daddy, are you upset about that little girl's communion today?" That malapropism might have brought a laugh in another situation. Anyway, I asked, "What little girl?", and Maddy said, "You know, Lindsay." I looked at Lisa, who mouthed, "Haven't said a word." So, we all had a long talk about death, dying, life, loving, etc. There were a thousand questions, most of which we fumbled though pretty well. But, this is not the story. The story lies in what Jim taught me through 18 months of ongoing communications about Lindsay.*

As I put Maddy to bed, she asked if we could have a Talk Time. Talk Time is a ritual that I assume happens throughout the world at bedtime. I crawl onto Maddy's bed, and we talk—about whatever—it's that simple. That night, she wanted to talk more about Lindsay. She asked, "does Jim have other kids?" to which I said, "Yes, he had four kids, but now he has three." Then, I quickly corrected myself and said "Maddy, actually, Jim will always have four kids, it's just that now Lindsay will live in his heart and his mind, instead of being together like we are now." While she was pondering that, I asked her if all this talk about dying was upsetting her. She sat up and said, "No Daddy, actually it makes me feel better knowing that if I ever die, I'll always be with you in your heart and mind." While I almost burst open, I also found a strange peace in those sage words from a five year old.

Heading into each fall, the PMC staff downshifts into a reflective, if not self-critical, mode. A few weeks after the weekend in 2011, some 1,700 riders responded to the annual survey. Starr and Hellman, the low-key operations director, eagerly culled through the feedback looking for any trouble spots to improve upon.

Using search terms like "hamburger" and "family finish" to find comments on snafus, Hellman said one relatively minor complaint was a long food line at a key site, apparently the result of a volunteer coordinator's absence, someone who typically regulates the portions allotted for an item to keep things moving. Even a small breach like that would be fixed to meet the goal of providing riders the service and total experience they expect. In the next week or so, Hellman would send a link to each of the PMC's volunteer coordinators—people like Cindy and Jon Chase—so they could search riders' comments and drill down further on their own.

For his part, Billy immediately shared two slices of feedback with me: service issues at the family finish area, and some riders' complaints that media coverage of the weekend didn't always convey its full emotional scope. A moment later, Starr rattled off plusses: overall luck with the weather, money's up, the Lance buzz, WCVB's large market share. Maximization of all inputs. "We are a bubble of affluence in a down economy," he said, his arms stretched cradling the back of his head. "That's my report."

Then he slowed down and began to wax philosophically on why the PMC occupies such a place in people's crazy lives. He articulated it so distinctively that taking notes felt unnecessary; it was more vital to simply stop and hear him in full. His reflection did not seem to gush so much from his longevity, nor from a cumulation of the PMC's physical years. It seemed to spring more from riding karma itself. How the experience coincides with a carousel of each season's rotation. As Nancy Shepard and others know, on a bike you catch the waft of lilacs, you come upon a bursting white dogwood. On a fall ride before the last bronze-oaks have fallen you're right there, singular or not, aware of the wheel slowing enough so that you finally take it all in. It's in your rhythm.

That morning, getting coffee he met a first-time rider from a team that had topped its goal by $6,000. Another reinforcement, someone else's story waiting to be heard. Starr had worked the first decade from home "toiling in anonymity in an uphill battle" that appealed to his sense of challenge. The urgency and fight never left him. And he gained "credibility through repetition, endless repetition of a guy who wasn't going away," he expressed in an email. "A guy who was lit up by his mission and the belief that what resonated within me was a core passion or principal of the human condition...and I was right. God knows, I like to be right."

"Life goes fast," he said, resuming pace back in his office. People age and become brittle. They put up barriers, they're busy. After the ride it may be golf, the beach, football, winter comes. In the spring, they may start training, it's March, June, and then it's the weekend again. "The PMC fills a need," he said, and they continue to come.

Starr cannot possibly know what each of those needs are. But the possibilities still fascinate him. The loyalty and durability of some longtime

Grill station at a lunch stop.

volunteers committed to run their hub or water stop is one armful. Early on, Billy recruited and cajoled many people. Some just keep showing up, and he may never learn exactly why.

Just weeks after each bike-a-thon, Carol and Tom Thibert start hashing over ideas for next time with their troops on the Cape.

It's often the little things repeated countless times that make a big difference. Over cookouts at someone's house, these notions begin to percolate. "Even down to how we line the porta-johns up," says Tom, who's been mainly in charge of a water stop in Brewster (and prior to that, in Orleans) since 1986. Some 110 people help out at Nickerson State Park, perhaps 50 of those members of a core group who do much of the heavy lifting. It's gotten to the point, says Tom, an electrician, that "all I do is pick up the phone and say I need some help and people show up."

One year someone came up with the idea of spreading peanut butter on pretzels, which many riders love. To supply water more efficiently, a guy who works at a golf course borrowed a trailer and built a double-filtration system with multiple spigots. Maybe 20 years ago, Carol's mother initiated the practice of slicing cantaloupes off the rind in advance—it's easy to go through a dozen cases of those, 10 cases of bananas and maybe 800 gallons of Gatorade. They fashion cold facecloths from linens supplied by the summer camp where Carol does bookkeeping and billing. Their Nickerson stop, Carol preens, was the first along the route to hand out popsicles. "The water horse is the envy of other stops," she says. "The guys over there are already thinking of new ways to make it better and more efficient."

What riders experience there is another surge of energy. Clarence Clemons and Springsteen honk through the trees. Two women do a Jersey swamp-salsa greeting riders who pass through a balloon archway. You're swarmed by people offering water refills. Patriotic banners are bursting, this year's theme at Nickerson. There's always a new twist.

Carol was the last rider to finish in 1985, her first year. Inspired by a cousin who had ridden, she also had two uncles on the road crew driving close behind her, while her husband manned a stop stocked with about 200 water bottles and some bread loaves. Carol rode eight years total. And then in 1996, Tom found a lump in his neck just two days after the PMC. He had an egg-sized tumor near his glands. He called Billy, who gave him a contact at DFCI, and soon began an experimental radiation protocol along with 25 other patients. Tom came through it. "It was done, but it was hell," he says. "I told my wife, we're going to run this water stop until they find the cure." They already had friends and relatives who had suffered, and there would be more.

Thibert briefly weighed the risks of joining the experimental program. Five doctors warned him, "We almost have to kill you to cure you." That night, he peeked inside the doors of both his kids' rooms, watching his son, then nine, and his 13-year-old daughter. And he knew. "I have to take a chance. Their lives are too important to miss out on anything."

On the last day of work before starting treatments, Tom was driving through Brewster when a warm sensation filled his body. "I still know the same place, all of a sudden a smile came over my face, and something told me, *I'm going to be okay.*

"I do talk to God a lot now," he laughs. "I owe him, I think."

Now young adults, son Sean and daughter Angela also pitch in each year. Their parents didn't hide anything about Tom's cancer from them.

When he came home from the hospital, they were easily involved in talking about things like his white blood cell count.

Each of the Thiberts have a job to do, made easier by every fresh or returning face. Jim Champion, in his 80s, helps every Saturday with the real grunt work pruning and cleaning the state park. A crew buys backup supplies like extra peanut butter and jelly or stuff not on the PMC truck. Another friend maintains his post each year, standing beside Route 6A guiding people in to the water stop. He always tells Carol, "This is where I want to be."

The wheel kept turning into another season.

One early spring night in 2012, Denise and I attend a new riders' orientation at the PMC warehouse. Arriving a little early, we check out tables stocked with shirts and caps, bike tool kits and glasses. Some are leftovers, plus there's plenty of free "schwag" takeaways like pens and key chains, so I grab two bumper stickers.

A PMC video with snippets of Billy's speeches over the years streams beyond rows of folding chairs. For those of us not already fully enticed, the session is meant to instill the full PMC experience: the expectations of self-reliance and preparation; offering assistance with the hard work ahead; and Starr's advice, ultimately, to unclip long enough to hear someone else's story.

Striding in wearing his black "Commit" t-shirt and jeans, Billy is at his best. He's supremely relaxed and grateful, at times holding his wrists, rubbing them gingerly as he talks. The forcefulness remains, yet he's rounded something more off his blunt edge than I've noticed before. When I introduce him to Denise, he remarks on how the March weather has been great, all the people out riding this winter. Naysaying prognosticators will predict a terrible July. We'll get our due, he observes, laughing it off.

"We're going to ask a lot of you, but we'll do a lot for you," he promises the 60 or so in our group as the 90-minute orientation begins. As first-timers, he advises us to put as much effort into the fundraising as we give to our training. He mentions a front-page article in *The Boston Globe* the previous day about donor fatigue and the stresses charity runners face in their fundraising. The piece focused mainly on the upcoming Boston Marathon. By a show of hands, many of us haven't read it yet. Ever on alert for demographic signatures, Billy probes how many still read the newspaper, in print or online. Most hands go up.

"I'm going to turn the tables on you," he blurts, dropping his hook. The writer interviewed Starr for the article, but did not use anything he said. I see that devilish smile curling. He flashes: the PMC raised more than 55 percent of the Jimmy Fund's annual revenue in 2011, and it generates 20 percent of Dana-Farber's entire budget. "The reality is that the PMC sits on the cutting edge of a $5 billion industry," he crows again. "What we've built is a synergy, an endurance event," not to be dampened by the tamped-down expectations of others.

As we dive into the nuts and bolts of preparation, I focus on phrases and chunks tossed out by Starr and his staff. Mentioning the 90-page event handbook, the PMC bible, Billy says, "The women will read it; the men won't even pick it up." He advises everyone to write these down, and we follow, the must-dos:

- Bring your cell phone in a ziplock bag
- Ditto for car keys if you're driving
- Your wallet with an ID
- Pack rain gear, unless there's an absolute guarantee of Arizona-like conditions

Next up, Michele Sommer, a new director of administration and a longtime rider, tells us about e-gifts and other donation-gathering tools. Dave Hellman continues this discussion, maneuvering the PMC website projected before us. After navigating through a couple of hiccups, Hellman spells out the text message being used for donations this year: "text pmc, your egift ID, to 20222." He walks through how to set up profile pages on the site, and adding links to social media. A training coach in shorts gives a crash course on physical preparation, advising us to cross-train and not to increase riding mileage by more than 10 percent each week. I feel that

Denise and I are okay so far, as we've been doing some 22-mile rides with almost four months to go. Optimally, however, he says we should now be working out four to six times a week.

The next speaker is a nutritionist, Charlie Smigelski, who courses through his primer. Most of this is new terrain to me, less so to my wife. He tosses out concepts like whey proteins, and the omega-3s in salmon and sardines, which he says are better than tuna because they have anti-inflammatory properties. He mentions repair proteins for riders, and easy-mix Gatorade. "Glutamine takes over where vitamin D and C run out," he says. A couple of times Smigelski snorts, "Your caveman genes are going to want..." Whizzing through a typical meal on a training day—there's even decent Chinese for lunch—he urges, "You might want a banana around four." He's got it all mapped out: your proteins, fruits and nuts, starch and juice for a four-hour ride (that's 4,000 calories for a 135-pound rider). He even suggests recovery-day foods. And before starting on the beer, he advises, drink lots more water. We buy his book afterwards.

There are a few more presenters. The volunteer coordinator is in full motion, as just over half of the desired 3,500 people have signed up so far. Glynn Hawley also seems to have his hands full overseeing provisions. Still wanted, he tells us, are a water sponsor, which means providing 3,000 free cases that fill two trailers; more sports drinks and soda; and 600 pounds of salmon burgers.

Starr returns in front of us to punctuate safety points. While some are just plain common sense, a few are new to our group. While the event has never been about speed, "I can't control how people ride," he tells us. "You need to be predictable and consistent. If you drop your water bottle and you're surrounded by a lot of people, *you really need to let it go.*" We laugh with his emphasis, though I can imagine my own foible ahead.

He clearly relishes some of these anecdotes. Not the one about a guy who didn't unclip and keeled over in the Sturbridge parking lot, separating his shoulder. But this one about joining "incidental draft lines" by riding extremely close behind someone. The grin is back. Falling in behind someone doing 25 miles per hour "and you're hoping the guy in front of you is as smart as you think you are." Ouch. That won't be us, we flinch. Billy's rules and courtesy tips become cycling mantra. Be spatially aware. Practice clear chatter. *Car back. Sand ahead. On your left.* Good defensive thinking. Don't go far outside yourself. And as he wraps up, Starr urges everyone, "on PMC weekend, take the time to meet a stranger." Smell the roses.

We start extending our rides, and I try to learn not to push my partner too much in all this. I take a light run one Sunday morning and then we go riding, still early enough to largely miss any traffic. It's bright with some wind leaning in from the southeast. Kids play in their yards. A man reaches to free his daughter's balloon, snagged in a tree limb. Our rural route passes dairy farms, the East Middleboro 4-H barn, where there's a heave of fresh manure. Forsythia bushes are butter-popping unblemished and workers are out on some of the bogs. My mother's magnolia flutters with a full luster in front of our house.

I won't wear the proper shorts yet, always out of fashion, but there's time. We check and it's been only 18 miles. Soon we'll cover a little more ground. A perfect and settled start.

A t least once, Meredith and Billy's friends pulled one over on him.

A year and a half before Starr's 50th birthday in 2001, his wife began plotting. One of his favorite places is Fryeburg, home of the Indian Acres Camp where Billy, his brother Mark and many cousins and friends spent summers in the 60s. It's the same place where his dad met Jay Ginns, the former counselor who would look after Milton during the war.

In a photo showing Billy as a camp counselor at perhaps age 17, he's muscular, almost barrel-chested, tanned, wearing tight white sports shorts, standing with a dozen campers beside a canoe. Surely he rode herd over them. Janet Ginns recalls that at times he also pushed the button of the camp director. "He used to drive the owner crazy because he didn't always do what he wanted," she says. Janet and her husband kept a summer house nearby at Kezar Lake. She remembers that after they closed it up, Billy

The Starrs with daughters Sophie and Hannah in 2000.

occasionally would ride over on his bike, bring a sleeping bag, and sleep out on the porch. Then he'd hike the next day. Starr grew so attached to the area he once dreamed of becoming Fryeburg's mayor.

Meredith asked the Indian Acres director about renting it out for a party. He turned her down, but she called again the next year, imploring him to think it over. "I knew it would mean a lot to Billy," she says. "Once in a lifetime." He finally relented.

Starr's 50th birthday was in April, and it passed without a major event. A few months later he was traveling to a race on Mt. Washington with a friend, who feigned nervousness and got Billy to take a detour. They drove east of Conway into Maine. Meredith had pulled it off.

After the season ended, Meredith and Billy's family and friends took over the camp, with nearly 200 people attending the party. They enjoyed catered food, softball, tug-of-war, canoeing and hiking all weekend. It was a true surprise. Meredith even had a band perform late into Saturday night, The 12:01 Blues Band, once a PMC staple. It was just about two weeks before the September 11 attacks. Years later, one of the band members told her, "That was like the last weekend of innocence, my band and I talk about it. All these families [there] having a great time, a perfect weekend; we played all night, and who knew what was about to happen?"

Starr remains rooted in those early experiences at camp and on the Appalachian Trail, fastened to their values: endurance, building camaraderie, answering the pain. He calls this the gestalt, or essence, of who he is, the personification of an ethos that is the PMC. When he looks back into that mirror again, even approaching four decades later, some of his features remain relatively unchanged, his face taut with a healthy glow. At 61, Billy still tries to ride every day, often at lunch.

"It's not hard to be true to oneself, at least I don't think it is," he told me. "I didn't create the value system; it's just part of who I am. My point was simply that when I created this event, it was supposed to hurt. That was the whole idea. Who wouldn't want to ride 200 miles?"

"One of the reasons I have been able to be as aggressive as I am is that I have always believed that 'to have the ability to ride this event was its own blessing.' Whether it was sports, endurance or goal-setting, I have always valued reaching for the extreme of good and goal-setting."

There's always the next roller to watch for, a fresh challenge ahead. Starr believes the PMC's course is secure, even as it faces considerations for sustaining growth. By 2010–11, its contribution to Dana-Farber was again growing while some notable multi-day athletic events were shrinking. The six percent percent gain in 2011 even wowed Billy. Then he and the trustees set a public goal of $36 million for the following year, while internally Starr figured PMCers would beat that by a million dollars. He nailed it.

Without a doubt, there are pressures and other measures to closely monitor: the rate of increase in new ridership has flattened; how to gradually replenish the PMC's bevy of top donors; and bringing in more of the next generation by offering other shorter routes with lower minimums, which the organization is doing. Other ideas to keep the event growing are on the table. One strategy advised by a growth study commissioned by the trustees is doing more corporate outreach. Some of this involves bringing in more young professionals and "targeting individuals in affluent networks." While doing so, the study notes, the PMC must also hedge against critiques of being an elitist event. It can do more to expand participation among people of color and broaden its base in the cities. Joel Bard, the Team Huckleberry rider, also would like to see the organization develop direct supports for unstable families going through cancer. Those unlike Hannah's, who lack the functional tools to cope.

There's more work to do. Yet Starr offers that anyone overly concerned about these things—or with donor fatigue, itself perhaps more a self-deflating construct than a reality for the PMC's core constituency—misses the point.

What's being generated to fight cancer is valued more than ever. By participants from every angle, need and background. The culture Starr spearheaded to "make it personal" thrives. Riders' average commitment grew by about $400 over three demanding years of 2009–2011 while average individual donations also gained. In-kind donations of goods and service from companies continue to soar. "We've been through three recessions and continued growth in two," he says. "There are no development issues. There isn't a reason to change the model."

Bold spices are continually added to that special sauce. There are continued improvements in fundraising tools and ways to give online. More children take part with their parents, as PMC Kids Rides already engage 5,000 youths in about 35 communities. Twenty percent of the event is under age 30. There's DFCI's name recognition, the PMC brand on Cape Air flights, the Green Monster, and coming soon to your local franchise. The ride continues as a manifestation of those attributes that first attracted Starr and his long-trekking pals—travel, speed, reflection, their energies poured out and yet still extant. The glass, he contends, is always at least half full.

There is one delicate issue on the horizon, though. It's the matter of restricted versus unrestricted giving to DFCI. Connections to loved ones are so visceral that an increasing number of people want to fund a cure for the specific disease that ravaged their lives. What this means to them transcends words.

Brent McCreesh's family in Southport, Connecticut, is among this group.

His dad Mike hadn't ridden a bike since he had a paper route as a kid, until their family was rocketed into a universe far from normalcy. Their trajectory thrust the McCreeshes and Brent's riding team to the front lines seeking a cure for neuroblastoma.

Dusty blonde-haired Brent was just a toddler when he was diagnosed on September 13, 2004. It was his first day of preschool, but by that evening he was at the nearby Yale-New Haven Hospital. Brent went from constipation a week before to feeling lethargic and then practically passing out that afternoon as tests were performed. "Overnight," his mom Dana says, "our life went from play dates and nursery school to chemo and blood transfusions."

Mike McCreesh, who works as an equities client manager at Goldman Sachs, wanted an explanation of what the numbers meant, the white blood counts. They learned that neuroblastoma was one of the most merciless childhood cancers, and Brent was Stage IV. With his specific diagnosis he had 30 percent odds of survival. A doctor told Mike something he'd never forget. While there might be 10 other patients like his son, he advised, "'When push comes to shove, there's only one for you, and only two numbers that matter: 100 and zero. And there's nothing in between.'"

After connecting with Boston Children's Hospital and the Jimmy Fund, Mike and Dana took action. Their son underwent seven rounds of chemotherapy, 13 surgeries, radiation, and hundreds of transfusions. He had two stem cell transplants, and a blue vinyl couch in 6 West at Children's Hospital became Mike and Dana's occasional bed. An erstwhile nurse named Caitlin Stratton, who since then has become a PMC rider, put stickers on Brent's bare head with Dana to help cheer him up. They made it fun as best they could.

Dana wasn't looking for new friends, but she needed help navigating this new place. Someone introduced her to Meredith Beaton Starr. Meredith met them at the hospital with hugs and coloring books, playing with Brent while his parents met the doctors. They recognized what really matters—it's not about vacations or fitness. "I remember using the time in the hospital to teach Brent about what was really, really important about life," Dana says.

"When we look at that time...we were amazed by the doctors and nurses, our friends, and family and everyone who made a difference."

Brent's health advanced after 16 months of treatments. The family began raising money for neuroblastoma treatment and research at Boston Children's Hospital and DFCI, and through the St. Baldrick's Foundation. (St. Baldrick's, the spunky nonprofit, has distributed more than $103 million for childhood cancer research grants since 2005. In 2012 there were 1,039 head-shaving events with more than 56,000 shavees. The foundation continued more than a dozen research and fellowship grants to DFCI and Boston Children's Hospital as 2013 began.) The McCreeshes sparked a formidable effort, raising more than $6 million in their first eight years, with about $3 million funneled through the PMC. Many of Mike McCreesh's Wall Street colleagues and friends joined in support of the cause.

TeamBrentWheels came about in 2005 as people kept asking how they could help.

Dana signed Mike up for the PMC over coffee with Meredith one day at the hospital. The only problem was, he didn't own a bicycle. He cried when she told him the number of miles involved. Then he called a friend, who loaned a bike. "I cried again. His bike had no pedals," he recalls. It had the clips for the shoes that most road cyclists use, which to him was like speaking Greek.

Mike's training for his first event was running up and down the stairwell at 6 West—at Children's Hospital—during the evening. He enlisted nine others, and it's been well worth the pain ever since. He still doesn't train that much. He makes a few 25-mile treks, does a little running, and declares himself ready. By 2011 his team had grown to 60 members.

Riding the first time for his son gave McCreesh his most powerful moment. He shared this memory with an audience of PMC donors in 2011. As he rode, Mike had a picture of Brent on the back of his shirt. He was about halfway through and struggling a bit when a rider came up, and simply said, "'Hey dad, how's he doing?' I said, 'Great.' As he rode away, he said, 'How about I ride the next 10 miles for Brent?' That was six years ago, but I think about that every day."

As Brent lives cancer-free he faces other challenges, including hearing loss and a growth on his liver. His parents also closely monitor other possible after-effects from his treatments. But as that summer of 2011 began, he loved nine-year-old things. Obsessed with soccer, he played five times a week and had four different soccer camps lined up. Dana would often catch him watching matches on Spanish stations. He'd become a Yankees fan, more loyal to his mom's side than to his dad's passion for the Mets. (The Red Sox remained in the hole, even as Brent loved going to Fenway Park.) An independent streak was flaring, as he prepared for overnight camp on Cape Cod for 10 days, where his older sister was also a camper. "He has no trouble being away from home," Dana said. She remembers the day he resumed nursery school after being with her for 15 straight months, including six at home in isolation when he was immunosuppressed. She worried how he'd deal with separation. "But he was ready to go, he walked right in. And for me, it was nice to go to the gym."

Brent's family, like Hannah's, continues to be lifted up by those around them who bring precious gifts, as the guy on the bike did for Mike in 2005. Together with their supporters and other families, who are often indelibly linked to the practitioners and researchers, they are modern legionnaires. It's a quest for the ages.

Mike McCreesh acknowledged to that audience of PMC donors that more training would make it easier for him to ride. "And it wouldn't hurt," he told them. "But the truth is I want it to hurt. It's the one weekend a year when I can take physical action against the disease. I go to the starting line, and I wage battle against neuroblastoma. And every year it hurts, but my goal is always to finish it. When I cross that finish line, I've kind of taken a chunk out of that disease."

These high-charged personal campaigns present a difficult balance for Starr. While appreciating and applauding such earmarked donations, from time to time he must gently advise against them.

The PMC's intent all along has been to provide unfettered funds to the Jimmy Fund for Dana-Farber to use at its discretion. Even a small shift towards designated funding can have big implications on what research and infrastructure gets funded. In recent years, the scales have been tipping a bit towards more directed giving, to almost a quarter of the PMC's total, with riding teams leading the charge. Although, they are neither encouraged nor discouraged from doing so, as with Hannah's team. "It is important that we don't lose sight of our original mission," Starr wrote PMCers in 2012.

Joel Bard does not restrict his donations as a Huckleberry rider, and he backs this flexible approach. In an email, he notes that "most of the big advances in cancer treatment have come from ideas that didn't necessarily jive with the scientific consensus at the time. Such ideas end up being hard to fund and the unrestricted budget provided by PMC is the sort of place that researchers can get money to do test those off-the-wall ideas that just might work."

Volunteer Sue Brogan agrees the gift Billy first rolled out is best when delivered with flexibility. "It gives these brilliant minds the ability to follow a path that they wouldn't be able to otherwise," she says, whether "in patient care or developing clinical trials or developing a process they weren't using."

While change is inevitable, Starr's confidence in how people will respond is resolute. "My big takeaway," he says, "is that the greatest value and cachet is that the PMC cannot be replicated. Therefore, it is absolutely worth it to belly up to the bar and join up, and make it part of your life."

Three days after the August ride Billy emails me: "How was your PMC?"

"Phenomenal," I gush. Denise was terrific, her stamina, and spirit. Both of us were exuberant, and we recharged along the route—emotionally, at least. Even more than we had imagined.

Little things have the most impact, some unspoken.

She stays close with a rider named Martha, mounting the hills in tandem. *You've got this Martha, you and I together.* Sensing she has just a little bit extra to give.

I meet eyes with people on lawn chairs. A dad surveys our group trickling by with a toddler crooked in one arm, a coffee mug in the other.

A costumed lobster dances as a woman plays the accordion beside him. I'm hoping for Zydeco gumbo, but it ain't spicy. It's more Lawrence Welk Oom-pah bubbles-polka.

We get a delicious cheeseburger head rush coming upon a group grilling beside their big signs in Rochester. Firemen in Barnstable out front with a massive flag suspended from a ladder truck as a shower begins. *Cool, cool rain.*

Rana gives us each a dog tag-style necklace as we meet Hannah and several Huckleberries at the Pedal Partner stop. It reads, "Thanks for riding to make a difference in my life!"

We come up a knoll. "I'm tired already—I've been here since 7!" a white-haired man guiding riders yells. Looks as if he's been grinning through five cups of coffee.

"It takes all kinds," a guy next to us retorts.

"Plenty of comedy routines," I chime in.

We overcome our trepidation of crossing the Bourne Bridge. Denise's dad Carroll, who for years supervised maintenance of state roads on the Cape, stands outside the rotary below the bridge chatting with a volunteer. Chatting really fast because he hasn't had his breakfast yet.

We follow a guy in a pink tutu from Eastham on. His apparel was the result of having challenged someone to donate, who responded, "Yes, if you wear a tutu." He keeps saying this one is the last big hill. Until we're ready to run him over.

Riding beside another first-timer, a woman with an Australian accent who now lives on Nantucket. She observes, this is the way life should be. Parents outside with their kids. Simplified. People giving back even a little of their time. *Isn't this really what this country is about?*

Pass popular Channel 5 anchorman Ed Harding in Wareham just before the Narrow's Crossing restaurant. We're meeting friends there and I want to ask Ed in to join us for a beer. Harding is riding for his second year. But he looks pretty concerned and has stopped. Maybe *he's* waiting for his wife. Watch a guy in a Viking helmet down a shot instead.

Kim, riding for Kara, perhaps a friend, we don't know, whose picture is on her back. She's rail thin, clumps of tangled Bonnie Raitt hair, her first time all the way to P-town. We're behind her for quite a ways and greet her later. At the finish, her mom is there, and they celebrate two big, fat anniversaries. Mom, who came in from St. Louis, is now cancer free; Kim is riding for the fifth year.

Two moments: Leaving the Pedal Partners' stop, all those kids struggling with disease, hits Denise. Such fighters. It sinks in, and we resume slowly as the road cuts into the woods.

For me the great lift comes in Brewster. Just past Da Hedge, where teens and younger charges are rising from behind the long shrub row, a mass emphatic voice, lifting and pounding, unrehearsed and yet repeated for each cluster of riders, each fresh wave. Just past them an equally boisterous group with adults are on the opposite side, rallying, continuing the

Denise Brack in Wellfleet, remembering her mother-in-law.

kids' energy. As I go past a man reads the back of my shirt, and sees her face on the button. "Riding for mom. Great!"

Both our dads meet us at the finish. We insist, let's head down to Commercial Street for a beer. It's on me.

The next morning I go pick up our dogs at the kennel. Coming back, on the radio there's Paul Simon, singing a song that forever makes me think of my mother. As a young child I circled the bases to this refrain, tracing a looped pattern of the rug on an uneven wood floor:

> *Homeward bound,*
> *I wish I was.*

For Hannah, something near normalcy emerged as the seasons spun forward.

Her readjustment took time after returning to school in April. She needed to find a niche among the girls' cliques in class. Flowing long hair was already in vogue, but hers was still short. Knowing that her daughter gravitated more towards boys anyway, Rana remarked, "She was better off when bald in some ways." Play dates had resumed. "But not enough," Hannah pretended to grouse as her lips formed a smile. "Only once or twice a month!"

Just in time to kick off summer vacation, Hannah's parents were wowed again. She'd already cleared a key benchmark, doing well a year after the transplant. "They look at that as a big step in the right direction," Jeff said. "They say about 80 percent of kids who relapse with Philadelphia Chromosome positive-ALL do so within the first year. That enhances it in our favor, but it can still come back." In mid June her latest test for the chromosome was negative again, and Hannah came off her medication.

Jeff and Rana could begin to reflect. "It's hard to tell anyone when bad things happen to your family that good things will come out of it," her dad said. "It's hard to realize that at the time, but it's true."

There would be more nail-biting and tests to clear. Yet, she was able to again enjoy a summer filled with play dates, swimming lessons, and even picking up sea creatures on a rocky beach. Hannah and her family pursued their summertime passion again, camping, which often took them to nearby Lake George. They drove to New Hampshire in their RV one weekend to help one of Rana's best friends. A former college roommate, she had traveled to Ballston Spa often the year before helping Rana during that stretch of isolation and hanging out in the backyard. She had recently had a baby and was going to a wedding with her husband, so Jeff and Rana combined babysitting with a little camping. For Hannah, there was also photography and theatre camp, and preparing to audition for the upcoming *King Midas*.

Team Huckleberry gave an encore. On another Thursday morning, August 2, 2012, they started the PMC weekend from the Hughes's driveway.

Returning was a natural, and vital. Bard, for one, was especially sensitive to the need for continuity. His cancer was a liquid blood-borne tumor like hers, and when the Hucks had met Hannah a year before, "everything looked great, but everything was on tenterhooks," Bard said. "There was a stage where the cancer might still be there waiting to come back, and you might not detect it. It just takes one T cell to survive sitting there dormant and conditions are right for it to start dividing again. When we saw her it was great, but still not 100 percent sure."

"I think there's cause for optimism," he said.

The Hucks presented Fiona with her own special gift, a necklace with a life preserver charm, a pendant Dave Grossman calls a "lifesaver." Setting off for P-town, the team would do a total of 380 miles in four days. Modifying their route to avoid dirt roads this time, they added a few miles and a lot more climbing. Some suffered severe cramping as they fought to stay hydrated. But they insisted on riding for Hannah again.

Her family, too, swept through Massachusetts again that weekend to rejoin the team at the Pedal Partner stop. First though, there was one more thing to do.

Before the Huckleberries rode off, Jeff and Rana braced to give her the purple cap and gown.

Epilogue

Some 5,454 PMC riders and 3,100 volunteers withstood the tough humidity and heat on PMC weekend in 2012, completing 800,000 miles. According to Starr, 19 riders went to hospitals including one who required surgery for a broken hip. About 80 Pedal Partners and 321 Living Proof riders participated. Retired U.S. Army General George Casey Jr., former commander of multinational forces in Iraq and a resident of Boston's South Shore, delivered a keynote address at opening ceremonies. On the eve of his second ride, Casey remarked on the parallels he found among the spirit in the military and how PMCers seek to make a positive difference.

Matt DeLuca, Mickey Ahearn and Nancy Shepard were among those riding again. DeLuca downed 21 water bottles "and still wasn't hydrated," yet he remarked that it was all great. He kept cruising at about 17 miles per hour. Matt mentored two younger men and saw the event anew through their eyes. Mickey was glad to see old friends once again during his 32nd PMC.

Riding in her 13th year, Shepard expected to hit $200,000 for her cumulative contribution. She took pride not only in that, but also in the knowledge that her daughter was volunteering for a ninth time at the lunch stop, where her husband also was assisting for his third year. "So it's become a whole family affair for us," she said. Nancy had also just begun working as a hospice volunteer assisting a woman with cancer, finding another way to connect with the challenges many people face.

A few weeks later, Hannah, Fiona, and their parents went to Disney World and enjoyed a cruise sponsored by the Make-A-Wish Foundation. The girls marveled at the giraffes outside their hotel room and swam with dolphins. Aboard the ship they received a private cake-decorating lesson from a head chef. Then as school began, the entire family settled in. Rana watched Hannah find her groove again academically and socially, feeling comfortable in her own skin as a fourth grader. One day while driving together, Hannah told her mom, "I'm so happy with my class, and I love my teacher." Fiona likewise adored her first grade teacher as that quintessential year rolled along. Sandy Fitzgerald continued to volunteer at their school, cutting back to three times a week because her mother was ill. She still kept a desk beside Hannah's, but didn't really need to. Hannah's nervousness was gone, and "now in the hallways she has a gleam in her eyes," her grandmother said.

Hannah's progress continued. Her first test results after coming off the medication were excellent, and her doctor said Hannah was in continuing remission. Visits to Albany were limited to about once a month, and hopefully they'd need to go to Dana-Farber only for a yearly check-up "She's been doing really well," Rana remarked before the holidays, "each day getting closer to that five-year mark."

Lance Armstrong's denial ended, but he cherry-picked the truth. He was officially banned from the sport, and the U.S. Anti-Doping Agency stripped his seven Tour de France titles. Armstrong resigned from his charity, which since 1997 had raised nearly $500 million to fight cancer, as the Livestrong Foundation dropped him from its name. Early in 2013, he admitted to Oprah Winfrey that he had used performance-enhancing drugs and bullied former teammates. He left open the possibility of trying to compete again by cooperating with the USADA.

In November of 2012, several days after the super-sized "Frankenstorm" ravaged a huge swath of the Northeast, Ed Benz looked out at South Boston's revamped waterfront. Few remnants of Hurricane Sandy remained on this crisp, calm Sunday morning. He thanked a crowd of PMCers for helping overcome what he called a perfect storm threatening cancer research. They had raised $37 million in 2012, a 5.7 percent increase, their biggest gift in 33 years. All official expectations had been exceeded.

Even so, Dana-Farber's need for the event's support was perhaps more dire than ever. Slashed federal spending on cancer research was the leading edge of the storm Benz referred to. A seven-year decline in funding from the National Institutes of Health made grants harder to obtain. NIH-sponsored research grants awarded to the DFCI/Harvard Cancer Centers had fallen from 481 to 467 the previous year. The coming federal budget sequestration amounted to another protracted hurricane season. Coupled with that were the demands of national healthcare reform, and his own state's attempts to control healthcare costs. Each of these forces pressuring his institution, like other comprehensive cancer centers, to allocate less than it would like for research.

Dr. Benz was on hand for his 12th ceremonial check-passing, this time at the Legal Harborside restaurant. He stood near a raw bar as supporters scooped up oysters and shrimp. Waiters circulated with trays of Bloody Marys and orange Mimosas. On the third floor, couples and families surrounded a sushi bar big enough to float an eight-foot dory. A few dozen including Billy had ridden their bikes into Boston and posed for pictures on the deck in their riding gear. Some local luminaries breezed through: New Balance CEO Rob DeMartini, Stacey and Larry Lucchino, and Channel 5's Ed Harding. Billy's brother Mark caught up with his aunt Betty and cousin Alan Starr. Senator Scott Brown stopped by early and soon dropped from sight, his campaign bus heading down Northern Avenue.

As he often does before audiences of PMC donors and participants, Dana-Farber's chief executive summed up the benefits in his direct and gentle style. New drugs are harnessing the power of the immune system to reject cancer cells. Fundamental research increasingly informs scientists "about the tricks that cancer uses to resist us," Benz said. Trials have examined genetic mutations that activate signaling pathways, which promote uncontrolled cell growth and tumors. He could hardly compliment the audience enough. Quite often, their donations made research possible before it became eligible for government funding and other grants.

Benz kept it simple, if not a tad corny: "I told a friend of mine, that because of you, the war on cancer is going to be won by bikes."

While Billy expected this latest surge in the PMC's giving, it came in a way that not even he could have forecasted. He'd actually budgeted for the record $37 million. But when ridership grew by only one percent, he thought the goal might be in jeopardy. Two-day riders provided the lift, raising their average contribution to more than $7,600 each. They had increased that average by about $1,000 during three years of a downturn.

Starr kept looking forward. A few days before the check presentation ceremony, as Sandy bore down on New Jersey and New York, he was ebullient as ever over the phone. "We know we have a ways to go to grow this event," Billy said. Weeks later, approaching Christmas, he peeled back another layer. The PMC's revamped web site was about to announce an official $38 million goal for 2013. "But that doesn't mean," he offered, "I'm not thinking we may do $39 million or more."

Acknowledgments

I thank Billy Starr foremost for his verve. It is inspiring on a very high level to spend some time with a person so unrelenting in fulfilling a vision that brings hope to so many. I am indebted to both Billy and Meredith Beaton Starr for their patience and repeated input with this book, which raised my learning curve and drove it further. Much appreciation also goes to members of the PMC staff, primarily, but not limited to, Dave Hellman, Alex Smith, Glynn Hawley, and Sarah Mercurio, each very welcoming, knowledgeable and helpful.

Rana, Jeff, Hannah, and Fiona Hughes all deserve a fitting round of applause. Beyond their strength as a family, I admire Rana's and Jeff's willingness to join the cause as Pedal Partners. Their openness to share their family's journey and their overarching grace is a compelling story of its own. To Dave Grossman and the other Team Huckleberry members, and all PMC riders, long may you run.

Other families and individuals who also give of themselves are especially noteworthy, including the Chases, the McCreeshes, the Rourkes, and the O'Riordans and Thiberts on Cape Cod. A shout out goes to all the volunteers, those untold and a few named, who make the bike-a-thon happen each year.

Of course, the dedication of medical practitioners, researchers, technicians and others at DFCI and the Dana-Farber/Children's Hospital Cancer

Center is at the core of this effort. I wish to especially thank Dr. Lisa Diller, Dr. William Hahn, and Dr. Ursula Matulonis, along with DFCI media specialist Robbin Ray. Nancy Rowe of the Jimmy Fund Golf program actually planted a seed that led me to Billy.

Several people offered constructive criticism, edits, and further context to help improve the writing. Those include Chris McKeown and Mark Starr, and the sweeping and valued edits of James Scott. Sound advice was offered by Judith Bradshaw Brown of the Davistown Museum, Stephanie Blackman at Riverhaven Books, and most critically, by her very thorough editor, Robin MacFarlane. Thanks to my sister, Jinny Brack, and my brother in law, Clay Block, who are both physicians, for their valued input on medical descriptions and much more.

In addition, Jim Coogan at Harvest Home Books gave solid tips on self-publishing options. Joining the Grub Street writers group in Boston has also been a godsend. My appreciation also goes to Jackie Herskovitz Russell and the staff at Teak Media Communications for the quick turnaround on PMC photos and other assistance. Thanks also to Wendy Semonian for her encouragement and blessing.

Most photo credits, including the cover images, go to John Deputy of Metrodesign, and PMC volunteer photographers. Others were provided by Team Huckleberry members and by DFCI, except where otherwise noted. My most enthusiastic thanks goes to Jeff Walsh for his cover design

Billy and Meredith leading yoga beside the Cape Cod Canal.

and customized Hucks' 2011–12 route map, and to Karen Alves of Design Principles, for her generous assistance with the covers, and taking the author's photo. Ryan Skerry also assisted with the map.

To my father, Robert Brack, who took care of Joan to the end, there are no adequate words. For my children, Mike, Chris, and Amanda, a piece of each of your resonates in this book.

Most keenly, I am indebted to my riding partner, my soulmate, Denise Fonseca Brack.

Notes

Chapter 1: Lovefest

1 "I want you to know": Billy Starr, "Billy Starr: My Road to the PMC," PMC Opening Ceremonies, 2009. Pan-Massachusetts Challenge web site. http://vimeo.com/5978877

2 "Together they speed the development": Robert, Levy, "The genomics decade," *2011 Spring/Summer Paths of Progress,* Dana-Farber Cancer Institute. Retrieved July 30, 2012. http://www.dana-farber.org/News-room/Publications/The-Genomics-Decade.aspx

3 "Practitioners call it": "PMC on CVB: The Doctors, Funding Research at Dana-Farber Cancer Center," *Chronicle*, WCVB-Boston. Broadcast August 3, 2012.

3 "A Connecticut couple whose son": TeamBrentWheels, Pan-Massachusetts Challenge web site. http://teambrent.com/pan-mass-challenge-pmc/. Also telephone interviews with Mike and Dana McCreesh, May 11–12, 2011, and August 22, 2011.

9 "The division did not participate in D-Day": Martin Blumenson, "World War II: The Liberation of Paris." Historynet.com. Originally published in *World War II* magazine, June 12, 2006. http://www.historynet.com/world-war-ii-the-liberation-of-paris.htm (Retrieved Oct. 26, 2012)

10 "The bells of nearby Notre Dame": Ibid.

13 "In the course of one's life": Billy Starr, Ibid.

15 "He approached the Jimmy Fund": Saul Wisnia, *The Jimmy Fund of Dana-Farber Cancer Institute.* (Charleston, S.C.: Arcadia Publishing, 2002), p. 88.

17 "'To me she was an angel": Stan Grossfield, "Founder Starr is Pan-Mass Challenge's biggest wheel," *The Boston Globe*, July 29, 2009.

19 "I swore to Billy I would never do it again": Barry Kraft, "Barry Kraft: A Trail Blazer," *PMC Yearbook 1994*.

19 "That night he told his": Mel Allen, "Pan-Mass Challenge goal: find a cure for cancer," *Yankee Magazine.* July/August 2009. http://www. yankeemagazine.com/issues/2009-07/features/billy-starr (Retrieved Sept. 18, 2012)

Chapter 2: Creative Chaos

30 "He told them, "The lamp which you": Samuel Zoll, remarks at Billy and Meredith Starr's wedding, Aug. 18, 1991. Courtesy of Billy Starr.

31 "Zoll shared this memory": Samuel Zoll, letter to Billy Starr, November, 1998. Courtesy of Billy Starr.

Chapter 3: Riding for Hannah

48 "Early Hannah was given a drug": Buchdunger, Elisabeth; Zimmerman, Juerg, "The Story of Gleevec," Innovation.org. http://www.innovation. org/index.cfm/StoriesofInnovation/InnovatorStories/The_Story_of_ Gleevec Retrieved June 25, 2012.

48 "Funding earmarked by PMCers": George Demetri, "PMC on CVB: The Doctors, Funding Research at Dana-Farber Cancer Center." *Chronicle*, WCVB-Boston. Broadcast August 3, 2012.

53 "In June Hannah joined a community workshop": "Art fest at Ballston Area Community Center," *The Saratogian* (Saratoga Springs, NY), May 26, 2011.

Chapter 4: A Line Walking Together

55 "This began in the late 90s": Robert Levy, Ibid.

56 "Medical breakthroughs have become" Saul Wisnia, Ibid, pgs. 10-11

56 "In the summer of 1947": Siddhartha Mukherjee, The Emperor of All Maladies. (New York, NY.: Scribner, 2010), p.19.

56 "By the next winter Farber": Ibid, pgs. 32–34.

56 "In 2011 alone, the Dana-Farber/Harvard Cancer Center": Dana-Farber Cancer Institute 2012 Facts. http://www.dana-farber.org/uploadedFiles/Library/modules/dana-farber-2012-facts.pdf Retrieved Dec. 5, 2012.

57 "Diller says when people like the Hugheses": Lisa Diller, Remarks at Heavy Hitters Night, May 10, 2011, InterContinental Hotel, Boston.

57 "Starr once said, 'Stick is what'": Michael Winerip, "A mover and a shaker of money trees," The New York Times, August 2, 2009.

58 "I wish I got to know her better": Jothy Rosenberg, "Stirling Winder: Osteosarcoma claims another," Who Says I Can't with Jothy Rosenberg blog. Sept. 6, 2012. http://www.whosaysicant.org/cancer/stirling-winder-osteosarcoma-claims-another

62 "By one accounting, some 11.6 million": "2011 Run Walk Ride Fundraising Survey — Top thirty Programs by Gross Revenue," Run Walk Ride Fundraising Council. http://www.runwalkride.com. Retrieved May 8, 2012.

62 "The feel-good by doing movement": Anne Kadet, "Are Charity Walks and Races Worth the Effort?", SmartMoney Magazine, June 21, 2011. http://www.smartmoney.com/spend/travel/are-charity-walks-and-races-worth-the-effort-1306536923690/?link=SM_mag_inside#tabs Retrieved May 10, 2012.

63 "One project continuing into 2013": Dana-Farber Cancer Institute. Susan F. Smith Center for Women's Cancers, annual report to golf tournament supporters, October, 2012, p. 5.

63 "By honing in on the different": Ursula Matulonis, "Gynecologic Oncology Program at Dana-Farber," updates provided to author, September, 8, 2012.

63 "We've been able to identify several": Ibid.

63 "In the fall of 2012": Ibid.

63 "Our group is now running": Ursula Matulonis, email to author with further program updates, December 16, 2012.

63 "Meanwhile, Matulonis's clinical group": "Gynecologic Oncology Program at Dana-Farber," Ibid.

Chapter 5: PMC Weekend

77 "If Armstrong does not cheat": Chuck Klosterman, "The Lance Armstrong Conundrum," *The New York Times,* November 9, 2012.

81 "At least one biking team lends": "Bieber Fever Raises Awareness for Rare Cancer," Pan-Massachusetts Challenge blog, February 17, 2012. http://panmasschallenge.wordpress.com/2012/02/17/bieber-fever-raises-awareness-for-rare-cancer-pmcers-are-the-backbone-of-funding-for-research/ Retrieved Feb. 18, 2012.

84 "And she journals the next day": Rana Hughes. CaringBridge journal entry, August 7, 2011.

86 "A native son of Salem": J.M. Lawrence, "Samuel Zoll does at 76; led district court judges," *The Boston Globe*, April 27, 2011.

88 "One year, expecting once again": Matthew Brelis, "Cyclists pedal 194-mile route to raise $1M for cancer research," *The Boston Globe*, August 13, 1989.

92 "*Crippled but free. I was blind all the time*": Robert Hunter, "Help On the Way," The Annotated Grateful Dead Lyrics. http://artsites.ucsc.edu/GDead/agdl/help.html

93 "The Hucks, meanwhile, are": Dave Grossman, "It's Not About the Bike," Thank you letter to PMC donors, Team Huckleberry, 2011. Courtesy of Dave Grossman.

Chapter 6: Her Skip Returns

101 "Her mom discovered that": Rana Hughes, CaringBridge journal entry, Feb. 8, 2011.

103 "'I was not ready to talk about": Rana Hughes, Ibid, Aug. 30, 2011.

Chapter 7: The Wheel Turns

106 "Chris shared this with donors": Chris McKeown, fundraising letter to donors, August 1, 2002. Courtesy of Chris McKeown.

116 "By 2011 its contribution": Nicole Wallace, "Walkathons and Athletic Events raise more money in 2011," *The Chronicle of Philanthropy*, March 2012. http://philanthropy.com/blogs/prospecting/thon-fund-raising-events-speed-up-in-2011/32464 Retrieved May 8, 2012.

118 "One strategy advised by": PMC Growth Study, The Parthenon Group, Boston, 2011. Courtesy of Billy Starr.

119 "The foundation continued more": Childhood Cancer Research Grants, St. Baldrick's Foundation. St. Baldrick's.org http://www.stbaldricks.org/where-the-money-goes/grants/country/US/city/Boston/state/MA/grantPeriod/all/searchGrant/Search/ Retrieved. Jan. 7, 2013.

119 "He shared this memory": Michael McCreesh, remarks at Heavy Hitters Night, May 10, 2011, InterContinental Hotel, Boston.

121 "Joel Bard does not restrict": Joel Bard, email to author, June 24, 2012.

About the Author

Ken Brack is a debut nonfiction author and journalist who lives in southeastern Massachusetts. His forthcoming, full-length, narrative nonfiction book conveys the experiences of people climbing from catastrophic loss and trauma who transform their lives to inspire others.

Previously an editor at business publisher Reed Business Information, Brack also reported for newspapers in New England, including *The Patriot Ledger* of Quincy, Ma., and the *Kennebec Journal* in Augusta, Me. He has also freelanced for *The Boston Sunday Globe West Weekly, North Shore Sunday* and *The Phoenix's New Paper.* Brack taught high school English for seven years at TechBoston Academy in Dorchester, Ma. His web site and blog is http://www.kenbrack.com

Ken and his wife Denise own and operate a bereavement center called Hope Floats Healing and Wellness Center in Kingston, Ma. The nonprofit provides support groups, primarily for adults who experience the loss of a child, a spouse, or partner, as well as providing counseling and wellness programs. (http://www.hopefloatswellness.com) They created the center in 2008 in memory of their son, Michael Thomas Brack.

In 2012 Ken and Denise rode their first PMC in memory of his mother, Joan Haskell Brack, who died of ovarian cancer in 1999. Their donations are earmarked for ovarian cancer research led by Dr. Ursula Matulonis at DFCI's Gynecological Oncology Program. The author is dedicating 75 percent of the net proceeds from this book toward the cause. The Bracks registered to ride again in 2013.

23782463R00089

Made in the USA
Lexington, KY
23 June 2013